HYPERANIMATION

DIGITAL IMAGES AND VIRTUAL WORLDS

Robert Russett

British Library Cataloguing in Publication Data

HYPERANIMATION: Digital Images and Virtual Worlds

A catalogue entry for this book is available from the British Library
ISBN: 9780 86196 693 6 (Hardback)
ISBN: 9780 86196 654 7 (Paperback)

Published by
John Libbey Publishing Ltd,
3 Leicester Road, New Barnet, Herts EN5 5EW, United Kingdom
e-mail: libbeyj@asianet.co.th; web site: www.johnlibbey.com

Orders outside USA and Australia: direct.orders@marston.co.uk

Distributed in North America by Indiana University Press, 601 North Morton St,
Bloomington, IN 47404, USA. www.iupress.indiana.edu

Distributed in Australasia by Elsevier Australia, Elsevier Australia, Tower 1,
475 Victoria Ave, Chatswood NSW 2067, Australia. www.elsevier.com.au

Printed in Malaysia by Vivar Printing Sdn. Bhd., 48000 Rawang, Selangor Darul Ehsan

HYPERANIMATION

DIGITAL IMAGES AND VIRTUAL WORLDS

Contents

Preface

This book offers an overview of a new and expanded form of animation that uses advanced digital technology to create fresh and innovative works of art. It is not about children's entertainment or the type of cartoon imagery that is generally produced for the motion picture industry, but rather it examines a new genre of animation that is exploring alternative methods of expression in a free zone of artistic experimentation. The content of this book, unlike purely academic texts or popular surveys, is essentially composed of interviews with the artists themselves, those creative individuals who are actually shaping this new direction and who in their own words provide detailed information about their works as well as insights into our contemporary technological culture. In addition to their interviews, a variety of supplementary materials are also included, ranging from biographical information and personal essays, to synopses and numerous illustrations. Because technical language is sometimes used to describe new digital media, a glossary of terms has been included at the back of the text. The goal of the book is to create a readable volume of lasting value, to provide insights into the works of individual artists, and to make clear the brilliant achievements of this little known but immensely important form of computer-based animation. The book is also intended to function in a number of instances as a kind of preserve, a sanctuary that contains detailed documentation of concepts that were once realized, but because electronic and digital technology become quickly obsolete, can no longer be made manifest in their original form. Although they are now gone, the essence and theoretical underpinning of these once beautiful works live on and remain important, contributing to their makers' subsequent production as well as influencing other artistic achievements in the field.

I have chosen the term Hyperanimation as the title for the book because, despite obvious limitations, it is broad and elastic enough to embrace the works represented in this collection. The term also implies a connection to its predecessor; the fine art of Experimental Animation, a movement that began in Europe during the 1920s and that in large part prepared the technical and spiritual groundwork for the development of Hyperanimation. Indeed, many of the artists interviewed within these pages acknowledge the importance of Experimental Animation and cite the pioneering achievements of this movement as a significant influence on their own creative production.

Facing page: A real-time frame capture from *Ephémère* (1998), a VR installation by Char Davies.

Below: From *Maxwell's Demon* (1991), a digital animation by James Duesing.

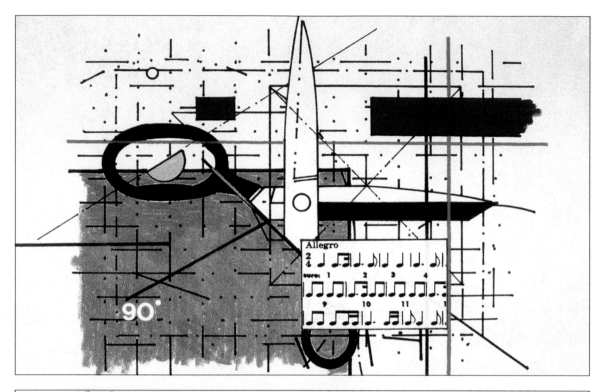

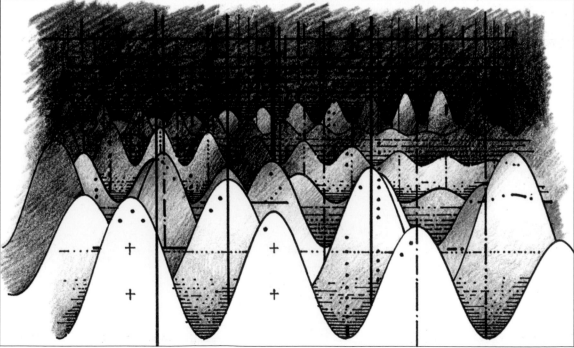

My wanting to compile a book of this kind sprang from a desire to examine in detail the significant artistic and technical achievements of Hyperanimation that have taken place in recent years. From my own experiences as a teacher, writer and media artist I have found that while the art pieces I have characterized as Hyperanimation have been covered peripherally in books and journals, surprisingly no one volume has brought this body of work to the forefront and recognized its immense importance as an emerging art form. There are, of course, numerous publications about computer animation, but for the most part they either cover technical and scientific forms of visualization, or they focus primarily on cartoon imagery, motion picture special effects or other kinds of commercial applications. Because of the apparent need for a concentrated and cohesive source of information about the subject, I began gathering material about those aspects of Hyperanimation that I felt would be useful to me, to other animators and media artists, as well as to critics, teachers, students and the interested public. I viewed my research, not only as the investigation of an exciting new genre, but as a continuation of my earlier research and writing about the genre of Experimental Animation, including an anthology co-authored with Cecile Starr that examined a seventy year span of this avant-garde film tradition.

As my research of the affects of digital technology on the art of animation progressed, I began to expand my activities, traveling extensively in the United States and Europe, conducting interviews and visiting galleries and museums as well as major research institutions involved with new forms of digital visualization. In evaluating the range and quality of the hyperanimated works being produced, I became aware that a new kind of art was developing, a highly energized form of expression that not only requires the artist to confront new technical procedures and creative possibilities, but also calls upon the viewer to develop alternative standards of judgment and at times even new aesthetic attitudes. As a result of advanced technology, the old methods of frame-by-frame film animation have been expanded to include a new level of synthetic imaging with applications ranging from interactive installations and digital theatre to virtual reality and telematic art.

With an aesthetic practice based on the exploration of new digital technologies and their evocative possibilities, Hyperanimation is clearly breaking new ground and demonstrating that it merits avant-garde status in several respects. It is advanced in that it has inherited from earlier avant-garde movements the aspiration to deny traditional artistic boundaries and it continues this commitment, developing works that explore new and expansive modes of expression. Hyperanimation is also advanced in the sense that it has immense implications for art and communication in the twenty-first century, addressing social and technological issues that have been scarcely sounded out in other quarters. And finally, the works produced in this new digital genre challenge the policies controlling our cultural environment and in particular call into question the current function of galleries, museums and the prevailing art and entertainment establishments.

Although this book contains a wide variety of information about many of the leading artists working in the field of Hyperanimation, it is by no means a comprehensive study but rather a representative cross section of the genre. For space reasons many artists who have made significant contributions could not be included, but undoubtedly scholars and historians will address their accomplishments in future volumes. My aim, notwithstanding certain omissions, is to capture in words and illustrations a broad overview of Hyperanimation and to present some of the most prevalent and current opinions in the field.

Facing page:
Upper: From *Object Conversation* (1985) by Paul Glabicki.
Lower: From *Under the Sea* (1989), a hand-drawn animation by Paul Glabicki.

Left: From *Wanting for Bridge* (1991), a computer animated film by Joan Staveley.

Right: From *The Morphogenesis Series* (2000–2005), a still image by Jon McCormack that explores the aesthetic possibilities of computer generated natural forms and plant-like structures.

It is also important to point out that the artists' interviews are presented in an historical context and reflect a brief but important period of time at the turn of the twenty-first century that signaled the emergence of Hyperanimation. While most of the artists interviewed have continued to produce hyperanimated works since they were first contacted, a few have changed direction or taken excursions into other forms of expression. To address the always-difficult task of keeping a book's content as current as possible, certain artists were queried a second time as the book neared publication. Therefore, while all of the interviews are dated, some interviews have two dates, indicating the addition of follow-up material.

The main body of the book's text is divided into eight chapters. Six of these chapters focus on specific subdivisions of Hyperanimation, separate directions that have emerged and developed within the genre. Essentially composed of interviews with individual artists, these six chapters are bracketed by an introduction at the beginning of the book that provides historical background material, and a concluding chapter that speculates about the future of Hyperanimation. Although the six chapters that contain interviews have a distinct thematic emphasis, they should not be construed as sharply defined categories, but instead as loosely formed divisions that have been created to facilitate analysis and indicate the formal diversity that exists within the field. Some of the artists interviewed in the book, for example, have produced works at various stages in their careers that could as easily be placed in one chapter as another, and in a few instances even classified as works belonging outside the pages of this volume. Hyperanimation is a fast moving and mercurial field, characterized by shifting perspectives as well as eloquence and innovation. The organization of the book, therefore, is designed not to isolate and rigidly define stylistic features and technical characteristics, but rather in a broader sense to explore the experimental mentality of the artists and the creative tendencies that energize their works.

There is no doubt that we are living in an epoch of global media morphosis and surely Hyperanimation, as a art form, cannot fail to face the changes produced by this transformation with all the faults, uncertainties and hopes that such a revolution brings. In this context Hyperanimation is only a provisional working title for a contemporary genre that will continue to take on form in and through a process of fundamental change in our society. The ongoing formulation of new ideas as well as the exchange of conflicting opinions are all part of this process. For example, the artists interviewed in the following chapters present individual perspectives and do not always agree with each other, but controversy is an essential part of the collective dialogue and ultimately contributes to the vitality, development and production of art works. With everything in flux and with technology advancing at an increasing rate, it would be presumptuous to describe Hyperanimation from a standpoint of completeness or solidarity. The discourse that takes place in these pages is open-ended, and openness is bound to remain a guiding principle in the future. It is in this sense that the content of the book is in part anticipatory. It is not just concerned with current forms of Hyperanimation, but with the prospect of opening up a pool of possibilities from which new kinds of artistic expression can emerge, operating at the edge of culture as an agent of cultural change.

Above: From *MEMB* (1993), a computer animated short by Robert Darroll.

Notes

In preparing for this book I conducted more than fifty interviews between the summer of 1999 and the fall of 2003, some of them in person, others by telephone or e-mail. Each of these interviews involved extensive research, including a close examination of critical and scholarly writings about the artist along with a review of as many of his or her actual artworks as possible. After careful consideration twenty-three of the interviews were chosen for inclusion in the book. I edited each of the selected interviews in order to put it in a concise and readable form and then verified each edited version by sending it to the artist for approval or correction. In addition to my interviews, I have also included a lengthy excerpt from a Rebecca Allen interview conducted by Erkki Huhtamo.

Most of the illustrative material that accompany the interviews in this volume – photographs, still frames, screen shots, diagrams, etc. – has been generously contributed by the artists themselves. Additional images have been provided by various individuals, archives and organizations (see *Acknowledgements*).

1 The origins of an emerging art

Animation isn't animation anymore.
– John Whitney

... The possibilities inherent in the relationship between new computational tools and artists provide a challenge that exceeds the powers of contemporary imagination.
– Robert Mallary

As we enter the twenty-first century, the growing presence of computer science, electronic imaging and telecommunications is producing profound changes in our cultural environment. These changes in turn are affecting our perception of the world and our methods of artistic expression. Recognizing the importance of this technological revolution and its immense potential, a new breed of innovative animators is redefining the fundamentals of motion graphics, developing new methods of artistic visualization and further extending the pioneering tradition of Experimental Animation[1] that began in the early years of the twentieth century. Although animation has long been considered a technique that generally consists of hand-rendered images recorded frame-by-frame onto motion picture film, new digital and electronic technologies have significantly expanded the definition of this venerable procedure. Since the mid-1980s an entirely new level of synthetic imaging possibilities have emerged, reinforcing the mutual tendencies of art and technology and ushering in a growing array of surprisingly powerful and expressive tools. These new tools have not only extended the technical range of animation, but are transforming the way we think about art and the communication environment that lies ahead.

The fine arts tradition of Experimental Animation essentially began in the 1920s with the probative abstract films of Hans Richter, Viking Eggeling, Walter Ruttmann and Oskar Fischinger, and extended to the more recent computer generated shorts of John Whitney, Stan VanDerBeek and Ed Emshwiller. Working within this tradition, a new generation of digital imagists has radically broadened the notion of motion graphics and redirected the effervescent field of Experimental Animation. Using advanced electronic and computational processes, these artists have not only produced an important corpus of work in a relatively short period of time, they have also prepared the underpinning for the flourishing of a new and dynamic audiovisual syntax, in effect, a form of Hyperanimation. The visionary works being produced by this forward-looking movement transcend traditional forms of expression and superficial uses of technology, and are the result of a balanced dialog between artist and machine. Contrary to much of the motion picture and television industries' current fascination with the "sensational" technical capabilities of computer imaging – often at the expense of substantive content – these artists-technicians are concerned with projecting a fresh sense of vision and creating compelling aesthetic experiences that explore new ways of seeing, thinking and feeling.

The Era of Experimental Animation

Initially the technique of film animation was largely regarded as a vehicle for entertainment, taking the form of cartoon imagery and a variety of "trick" effects.[2] However, artists and especially painters soon recognized that it had applications in their field and began to test the inherent perceptual and aesthetic possibilities of the medium. Indeed, in 1907, even before the movie camera could film one frame at a time, Italian painter Arnaldo Ginna conceived of a hand-generated graphic approach to cinema. In an article titled, *Abstract Cinema, Chromatic Music*, Ginna described in detail two years of experimentation that gave rise to a number of realized works. By circumventing the use of a camera and painting images directly onto motion picture film, Ginna created the first recorded genuinely abstract films. Although relatively unnoticed at the time these works introduced

Facing page: From Motion Painting No. 1 (1947) by Oskar Fischinger. [Courtesy Elfrieda Fischinger Trust.]

Top right: Oskar Fischinger, 1932.
[Courtesy Elfrieda Fischinger Trust.]

Below left: From *The Adventures of Prince Achmed* (1923–26), by Lotte Reiniger. Based on a story from the *Thousand and One Nights*, this work was among the first all-animated feature films ever made. [Courtesy Cecile Starr.]

Below right: Lotte Reiniger at work in her studio with a team of assistants. [Courtesy Cecile Starr.]

aesthetic level his animation was lyrical, sensitive and multisensory, employing a well-developed and interdependent audiovisual approach. This approach to his work can be experienced not only in the rhythm and pace of the visual forms as they move and transform, but also in the sequences themselves as they repeat like melodic units in a musical composition. Ruttmann's contributions to Experimental Animation were limited in number, but important in terms of their quality as well as their influence on other artists that were to follow.

Oskar Fischinger, who was the youngest of the four pioneering experimentalists working in Germany during the twenties, had already demonstrated a theoretical interest in a new abstract cinema by 1921. He had made a series of

Left: From *En Passant* (1943), by Alexander Alexeieff and Claire Parker. Illustrating a French Canadian folksong, this film was produced using pin board animation, a technique invented by Alexeieff. The subtle light and dark values that define the imagery of *En Passant* were created by manipulating the board's one million movable pinpoints, frame-by-frame.
[Courtesy Cecile Starr.]

Right: Alexeieff and Parker shooting illusory solids in their Totalization workshop (c. 1960). Animated solids result from the frame-by-frame recording of a moving tracer; contrary to all other film animation techniques the frame is exposed while the object is in motion.
[Courtesy Cecile Starr.]

abstract drawings and collected numerous articles about the subject, but had not yet actually produced a film. It was not until he had attended the premiere of Ruttmann's *Opus 1* that a marked change took place in his career. The screening of *Opus 1*, which he found extremely impressive, could very well have motivated him to begin practical work in animation. Between 1921 and 1923, Fischinger invented an animation device that enabled him to conduct experiments with abstract imagery. The device was designed to slice thin layers from a specially prepared block of wax that contained a conglomerate of colored shapes. The blade of the device was synchronized with a motion picture camera so that as the block of wax was sliced, gradually changing colors and shapes were recorded onto film. These works were followed by clay animation and various kinds of stop-motion films as well as a number of short experiments with abstract motion graphics. There is also evidence that Fischinger produced several multi-projection film displays – an early form of installation art – at his studio around 1926 and also showed films as part of *Farblichtmusik* (Color, Light, Music), a multimedia presentation staged by composer Alexander Laszlo. None of Fischinger's works from this early period survive in the form in which they were originally presented. However, much of the experimental film footage and graphic work he produced was preserved by his wife Elfriede and now resides in the Elfriede Fischinger Trust in Los Angeles, California.

The year 1929 marked a new phase in Fischinger's career. He became involved in animating a section of Ruttman's *Melody of the World*, then started his own enduring *Studies*, a series of black and white abstractions carefully synchronized to various forms of music ranging from jazz to classical pieces. It is for these works and the abstract animated films done after 1930 such as *Allegretto* (1936), *Optical Poem* (1939) and *Motion Painting No. 1* (1946), that he is best known. During his last years in Germany and later, after his arrival in America in 1936, Fischinger stood as an immensely important figure in the field of Experimental Animation, influencing several generation of artists including those who are now using digital technology to produce a new kind of motion graphics.

Also emerging in Europe during the twenties and early thirties were a number of independent animators who employed pictorial subject matter and narrative themes rather than pure abstraction. For example, the richly delineated and deeply

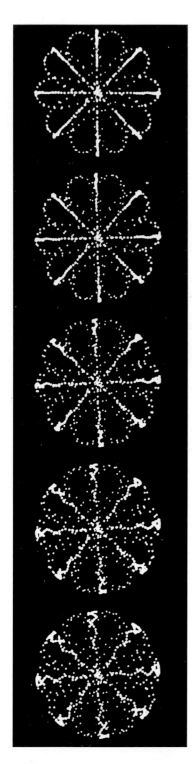

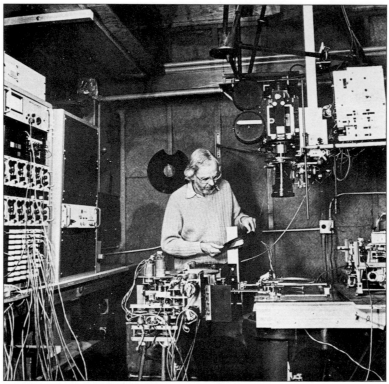

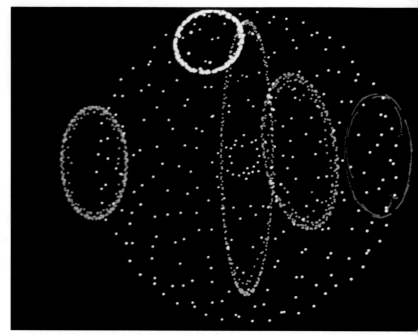

Left: Filmstrip from *Permutations* (1967) by John Whitney.
Centre: John Whitney in his studio with his mechanical analog computer.
Right: From *Permutations* (1967) by John Whitney, produced with digital computer equipment under an IBM research grant.

[These images courtesy the estate of John and James Whitney.]

addressing the specific needs and potential of dynamic digital media. The history of art has shown that this type of concurrent development in creativity and exhibition methods often occurs when new techniques are discovered and employed. Marcel Duchamp's rejection of "pictorial" modes foreshadows a contemporary trend in the arts that wants to transcend traditional forms and uncover deeper meanings by using dissimilar and experimental techniques. Photography, motion picture film, and then video demonstrated the power of advanced technologies to provide a vast new territory of artistic forms and display systems. Now digital computing, telecommunications and other electronic means of expression have opened up an even wider perspective.

To accommodate this evolution of media art, including the emergence of Hyperanimation, provisional approaches to the production and exhibition of works are being developed and tested in a number of locations around the world. Some of the predominant venues and research centers leading this new tendency include Ars Electronica Centre in Linz, Austria; the Center for Art and Media in Karlsruhe, Germany; the InterCommunication Center in Toykyo, Japan; and the MIT Media Lab in the United States. Also making important contributions to the field are the Electronic Visualization Laboratory at the University of Illinois (USA); the Center for Advanced Inquiry in Interactive Arts (CaiiA-STAR) at the University of Wales and the Banff Center for the Arts in Banff, Canada. The efficacy of these and other artistic initiatives will depend on the position they take in terms of education, production and presentation within a larger world of distributed information, including the universal realm of cyberspace. Conceivably, these emerging venues and institutions can be landmarks in the vast and varied creative landscape, stimulating artistic activities and contributing to significant changes in our cultural environment.

Because the digital art form of Hyperanimation has multidimensional and polysensory expressive capabilities, it often engages the viewer in unprecedented ways, using new types of interfaces and display systems. Unlike television and motion picture film, for example, Hyperanimation does not have to conform to a standardized format and projection system, but rather can be exhibited in a wide variety of forms and configurations. Interactive media, virtual reality, telecommunications, digital theatre and large-scale stereoscopic installations are among the types of expression currently being developed and used by this new breed of artist-technician. Possible future applications for Hyperanimation could involve nanotechnology and avatars, and could range from various kinds of telematic art that are transmitted via worldwide networks to immersive cybernetic spatial environments that affect the entire human sensorium. In effect, it could become a type of digital *gesamtkunstwerk*[4] that fuses the multimodal characteristics of numerous art forms into a unified aesthetic experience. It is impossible, of course, to predict the extent to which technology will bring about the fulfillment of these ambitious initiatives. Nevertheless, there is at the present time a real need to anticipate and examine their artistic potential and cultural significance.

Although the focus of Hyperanimation is on free and open artistic experimentation, the promising developments coming out of this new realm of synthetic imaging are bound to have a growing impact on commercial and practical forms of visualization in the years ahead. Science, medicine, the Internet and the entertainment industry are but a few of the many areas that are likely to be affected. The computer and other new technologies are expanding the possibilities for visual representation and opening up a whole new kind of communication among the artist, the audience and the kinetic image. Much is to be gained by recognizing the innovative work being produced in the field of Hyperanimation and the distinctly new form of artistic experience that is being created. However, because Hyperanimation is new and relatively undocumented, considerable research and analysis needs to be done before its full importance and far-reaching implications can be clearly understood. The issues being addressed and articulated by this new form of expression could very well alter our sense of perception; change our cultural environment and transform the way we think about art and communication in the new millennium. Although Hyperanimation is still at an early stage of development it is not too soon to examine rigorously the underlying theories of this new discipline, to try to define its boundaries, and to consider through its revelatory and arresting images, its enormous significance for the future.

Notes

1. For specific information about Experimental Animation see Robert Russett and Cecile Starr, *Experimental Animation: Origins of a New Art* (New York: Da Capo Press, 1988). For information on the subject, within the context of the entire field of animation, see

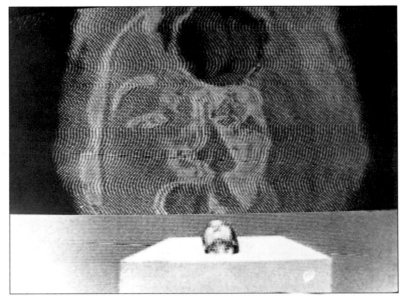

Left: From *Scape-mates* (1972) by Ed Emshwiller. In this work Emshwiller used real-time videographics, live dancers and computer generated environments to produce a synthetic world of surreal imagery.
[Courtesy Susan Emshwiller.]

Giannalberto Bendazzi. *Cartoons: One Hundred years of Cinema Animation*. London: John Libbey & Company Ltd. in association with Indiana University Press, 1996. Experimental shorts by pioneer animators Hans Richter, Walter Ruttmann, Viking Eggeling, Mary Ellen Bute, Lotte Reiniger, Len Lye and Alexeieff/Parker are available in the USA from Cecile Starr, 35 Strong Street, Burlington, Vt. 05401; e-mail Suzanne.Boyajian@verizon.net A selection of other experimental animated films, including works by Oskar Fischinger and John Whitney, are available from The Museum of Modern Art (NY), Film and Video Circulation Department.

2. The term "trick effects" is generally associated with early filmmakers (Georges Méliès, for example) that were fascinated with stop motion photography and used it to create unusual and amusing effects.

3. Eadweard Muybridge (1830–1904) gained worldwide recognition photographing animal and human movement. He developed a method of working that involved recording individual still images, which captured the progressive movements of his subjects. In 1887 he published 781 of his prints in *Animal Locomotion*, the first reliable scientific study of movement.

4. *Gesmtkunstwerk* refers to a synthesis or unification of all the arts – theater, music and pictorial representation – into a single medium of expression. In his 1848 essay, *The Art-work of the Future*, Richard Wagner stated that the future of music, music theater and all the arts lay in an embrace of *gesmtkunstwerk* or total art work, a fusion of the arts that had not been attempted since the classic Greeks.

Both images: From *Maxwell's Demon* (1991), digital animation by James Duesing.

because I'd heard they were doing computer art and invariably I'd see *Playboy* centerfolds printed out in X's and O's on the wall. I had also seen *Luxo Jr*, one of the more successful computer animations produced at that time, but felt that wasn't what I wanted to do either. I think the real reason I started animating *Maxwell's Demon* on the computer was because I realized there was a way to make animated images that I hadn't seen before and even though my plans for the production process were out of the main stream and extremely labor intensive, it didn't seem any more difficult and time consuming than having to draw every frame by hand.

Q: Would you discuss the technical evolution of your work with computer animation, beginning with the Cubicomp system that you used to produce *Maxwell's Demon*?

JD: Essentially, the technical evolution of my work parallels the evolution that happened in desktop computing. All of my computer animation, over the last fifteen years or so, has been done on various kinds of desktop computer(s). I worked on *Maxwell's Demon* from 1987 to 1990 and completed the postproduction phase in 1991. It was a time frame that coincided with the rise of PCs and independent computer animation, a period when 3D software and equipment was just becoming available.

When I started *Maxwell's Demon* I heard a lot of people saying one of two things: either that no one would ever make something on a desktop computer that could compare with what was being done with mainframe computers, or that all computer animation, because of the technology, tended to look alike. Of course, I didn't agree and there was something in me that really wanted to prove a lot of people wrong. One of the biggest obstacles in producing *Maxwell's Demon* was dealing with extremely small hard drives, which made it necessary to store all the images on 4.5-inch floppy disks. It was an incredibly labor intensive process and by the end of the project I had binders full of floppy disks with all the images from the animation on them. When I moved three years ago I came across all those binders filled with the numbered floppies. I couldn't think of where I could find a computer to put them in, and if I did the files couldn't be read by any available program. So I threw them all in the trash. Before the janitor could pick them up someone came by and took all the binders, but left the floppies.

By the time I was ready to start animating *Law of Averages* (1996), things had changed radically. I had a studio set up in my home and I was using very capable software: 3-D Studio and then 3-D Max. The next piece I did, entitled *Cultural Tourism* (1998), was an animated journal for the web. I did the entire piece on my laptop computer, most of it during a residency at the Headlands Center for the Arts while looking out over the Pacific Ocean. Recently, I produced a short called *Tender Bodies* using Maya 3D software, working back and forth between an SGI and a PC. In this project I used the web as a pre-production tool. I posted my storyboard and script as well as character sketches and rendered models. I'll probably have rendered sequences online eventually.

Q: *Maxwell's Demon* and *Law of Averages* are two of your better-known animated works. Would you comment on their visual structure and subject matter, as well as their political and social content?

JD: The visual structure of *Maxwell's Demon*, meaning its stylistic treatment, was at that time considered rather unconventional. I used 2D paint effects and flattened 3D elements because, for one thing, I wanted to make images that departed from the then prevalent style of computer animation. I wanted to show that the inherent qualities of work done by the artist's hand could still be discerned in the imagery, even though a machine was being used to produce the animation.

In terms of its subject matter, *Maxwell's Demon* takes place in an information and service-based economy; industrialists are corralled on a reservation named Lorado where they produce and sell various kinds of inane plastic merchandise. The reservation is built on a polluted lake, which is a tourist attraction. The story turns on the suicide of a pet fish belonging to Fashionette, a main character in the story. The fish's suicide was brought about by bad water conditions. Fashionette is a hot head and blames the pollution in the lake on Max, who owns the largest gift shop in town. When Max offers to buy Fashionette's dead fish with the intention of selling it as food, a confrontation takes place between the two and ends with a large-scale chemical fire that no one knows how to put out.

In *Law of Averages*, which is rendered mostly as 3D computer animation, the story unfolds in a lush garden. The temptation in this garden is an interactive theater called The Big Ghost. Vynola, an exotic bird-like creature, is the bawdy tour guide in this endlessly exciting cyber world. Destitute people, addicted to this entertainment, are frequently seen in the vicinity of the theater. Everyone has a place where they live, an open area sometimes defined only by a wall or two. They all have a couch and a TV because it helps them to 'think'. The Big Ghost is the only actual building in the garden.

As I developed this project it became clear that the key to this work was in the portrayal of the environment. It's an environment full of contradictions. For example, on the one hand it's a world filled with lush vegetation, but on the other hand plants and flowers are frequently personified as spewing pollen, eating things or stretching their stamens out to rub against each other. The intent of the piece was not to present a story with a happy ending, but rather to provide an allegorical look at the complex issues of contemporary life. I wanted to show imperfect characters making decisions about daily events while enduring the complications of technology, unhappy relationships and overly simplified doctrines for living.

As far as politics and social content are concerned, there are specific issues that are important to me and that shape particular works. However, because of the amount of time required to make an animated piece it's impossible for me to be topical. If I started a piece about a specific event or politician, by the time I finished it the thinking about that issue may be at a different place or another politician might be in power. I try, therefore, to make these animations devoid of any concrete references to specific people, places or objects. Yet, I try to make the characters emotionally complete and their environment complex and

Both images: From *Law of Averages* (1996), 3D computer animation by James Duesing.

VS: I became interested in digital computer graphics as an extension of my work with analog computers and video stereoscopy. The digital computer provided a higher degree of control over every aspect of the imaging process and allowed me to achieve an increased visual and temporal subtlety as well as an extended range of graphic effects. I was convinced, even during those early formative years, that digital media would revolutionize the form and content of pictorial expression.

Today digital computers have the conceptual prowess, memory, speed and algorithmic capabilities to produce complex polysensory effects that are coming very close to simulating many aspects of human perception. And as digital media develops, it will become possible to manage and exploit even more effectively the sensory modalities of sight and sound, creating fertile and exciting opportunities for entirely new kinds of stereoscopic experiences.

Q: As an artist, exactly why does stereoscopy interest you?

VS: I find stereoscopy an incredibly dynamic but very mysterious art form, notwithstanding all of the scientific research that's made it possible. For instance, when I view stereoscopic imagery I'm particularly fascinated by what I regard as a paradox in perception. Intellectually, I know I'm looking at two flat pictures that have a slightly different perspective, but experientially I see objects and spaces that convey a convincing realistic illusion of volume and depth. As imagery,

Right: Microfiche (1985), a stereoscopic still image by Vibeke Sorensen. In this composition, the artist plays with the language of technology, producing a digital image that is the equivalent of a witty one-liner.

stereography has a concrete presence with palpable physical characteristics, but because it is an illusory impression it also has a certain ethereal quality similar to music. When stereoscopic imagery is technically well executed, it can be a powerful and mind-opening spatial experience with a unique kind of expressive quality.

Q: In general terms, what is the underlying psycho-optical process that produces the stereo-scopic effect?

VS: In order to create a stereoscopic image using computer graphics, or any other technique for that matter, two flat graphic sub images must be made, one for each eye. These two sub images are of the same subject, of course, but vary to a small degree in their perspective. By looking at the separate sub images with a stereo viewer, or some other type of separation device, each eye will see its, and only its, perspective viewpoint. A phenomenon called stereopsis makes it possible for the brain to fuse these two flat sub images into a single picture that is perceived as having a real dimension of space. I find it surprising that the physiology of perception is rarely referred to in the study and discussion of contemporary art. It seems to me that a close examination of human vision and how it works would be especially helpful to artists who are involved with the development and use of new imaging technologies.

By its very nature the Art and Technology movement is interdisciplinary. Its growth depends on specialized research in a host of areas that don't normally concern artists who work with traditional media and techniques. And the physiology of human vision is certainly one of those areas. There is undoubtedly an important and inexorable link between our knowledge about perception and the development of technological art forms. For example, if during the nineteenth century the scientific community hadn't discovered persistence of vision and stereopsis we wouldn't have motion pictures and stereoscopic imagery today. Obviously in these two cases science provided certain essential information about the mechanics of vision that helped revolutionize our way of making and viewing art. In the future other aspects of our sensorium could be uncovered that further alter and expand our methods of perception and change our approach to the creative process. I'm convinced that the human visual system and psyche bear far more potential than we presently realize.

Q: Continuing with this line of thought, would you comment on Jacob Bronowski's views regarding the anthropological development of stereopsis? It seems his ideas could have some interesting implications for the future of stereoscopic imaging.

VS: I agree. If Bronowski's theories[5] are accurate, art and visual communication could become a very different type of experience in the years ahead. In his writings, he points out that although stereopsis has contributed significantly to the human evolutionary process, three-dimensional perception is still a relatively recent addition to the primate visual system. It is, in fact, according to Bronowski, a part of our physic ability that continues to develop. He theorizes that our capacity for three-dimensional perception is connected to some kind of cognitive process, and that every time this process is affected by new and stimulating spatial imagery, it becomes more developed and more functional.

Now that we know about stereopsis and are aware of its potential for imaging, we'll undoubtedly continue to search for ways to develop and use it. I believe that we have hardwired into our system an instinctive or innate urge to increase our technical capability for multidimensional and polysensory experiences. It's quite conceivable, then, that our knowledge of stereopsis will eventually lead to an advanced three-dimensional imaging system, just as the discovery of persistence of vision made the dream of motion pictures a reality. Should binocular vision evolve as Bronowski suggests, not only would our perception of the natural world be affected, but so would the dynamic visual range of computer space, an emerging world unto itself that is full of magical and expressive possibilities.

Right now researchers tell us that the resolution of three-dimensional binocular vision is about ten times as high as monocular vision. It logically follows, then, that three-dimensional images produced using stereoscopy, holography and the like, are capable of conveying far more information than two-dimensional images. I think this is an especially significant fact considering that we are currently in the process of designing and implementing an entirely new type of worldwide communication system.

The future of media and stereoscopic imaging in particular, will not only depend on the resolution of complicated technical issues, and there are many, but also on a deeper understanding of the structure and function of human perception and how it can be used most effectively.

Q: When did you begin to use stereoscopy as a form of expression?

VS: My work in stereoscopy dates back to 1978 when I produced my first stereoscopic film *Hot Wax*, along with a large number of stereo slides and stereo photographic prints. *Hot Wax* is a thirty-minute experimental animated work that was produced with an analog computer and then recorded onto 16mm motion picture film. At that time, I was working with equipment and processes that would be considered very primitive by today's standards. For example, I didn't use off-the-shelf software to produce the animated sequences for *Hot Wax* because, very simply, there weren't any graphic applications or animation programs available at that time.

When I began working with a new generation of digital computers in the early 1980s, some fundamental changes took place in my work and in my methods for visualizing graphic form. I found that the new 3D software that was being developed for digital computers was a direct descendent of photography and that it was modeled after the camera's capability for rendering detailed subject matter and perspectival space. Of course, a critical difference between photography and digital imaging is that a camera can only record what's there, while the computer, on the other hand, is like a paintbrush and can create imagery that never existed. In any case, these new digital computer systems and their 3D graphic software provided me with an opportunity for exploring a new and advanced form of visualization that was created by the intersecting attributes of light-based media, still and motion picture photography, and the powerful new 3D graphic techniques of the digital computer. In 1985 I made numerous stereo stills by photographing directly off the computer screen, including *Fish and Chips* and *Microfiche*.[6] Since then I've continued to produce stereo slides as well as stereo prints on a regular basis. From 1987–92, I created the *Reflection Studies Series,* a group of fifteen thematically related abstract works. And in 1994 I produced another collection of stereo slides called the *Earth Consciousness Series.*

Q: What, specifically, were some of the things you were doing with stereoscopic motion pictures during the eighties and nineties?

VS: One of the more interesting projects that I was involved in during the eighties was *The Magic Egg,*[7] the world's first 3D computer-animated film made for Omnimax Theaters. I produced a short segment for the film in which I used the NASA star database and James Blinn's software to animate the constellations, delineating the transformation of our old anthropocentric and anthropomorphic view of space to our current understanding of how the universe looks. Although *The Magic Egg* was not a stereoscopic project, it gave me an opportunity to gain valuable experience with 3D motion graphics, the same type of imaging technique used to generate the complex binocular effects for computer stereoscopic animation. Ever since my involvement with *The Magic Egg,* my interest in astronomy has continued and I often do consultation work for space exploration projects at the Jet Propulsion Laboratory. Recently, for example, I produced seven computer-animated scenes for the JPL, simulating the unmanned space probe to Mars and depicting how the mission will undertake the task of mapping the entire planet.

Interview with JOAN STAVELEY

Q: *Broken Heart* (1988) is considered by many as a pioneering film in the field of 3D computer animation. Would you provide some background about this work and discuss its genesis?

Joan Staveley: I made *Broken Heart* when I was a graduate student at Ohio State University. I'd received a BFA from the University of California at San Diego and then lived in Europe for about a year before enrolling in the OSU graduate program in computer animation. Although the idea of using computers to make art had interested me for some time, up to that point I had never actually produced any work with digital technology.

I found the first year at OSU very difficult. Beginning students were located in a freezing basement room of the Cranston Csuri Building using computers that were quite primitive by today's standards. All of the motion had to be programmed. There was no real-time playback and there were only 16 colors to choose from. We filmed our work frame-by-frame off the frame buffer and saw it a day or two later after the 16mm film was processed. Conceptually, I wasn't particularly interested in doing character animation like most of the other students, but rather wanted to explore more serious kinds of subject matter. By my second year I became technically more capable and began to find a creative direction for myself. In my hand-drawn animation class taught by Chris Wedge, I discovered that I already had a good feel for the basic principles of movement due to years of dance experience. Chris also showed us a wide variety of motion pictures, ranging from experimental works to animation, which gave me a deeper appreciation of the medium. I started to see the mastery in Bugs Bunny and other character animations, but it was the experimental films of Maya Deren and the animation of Susan Pitt that really impressed me. After seeing Maya Deren's *Meshes of the Afternoon*, I decided to turn to my earlier experience with dance, something that I had been very involved with throughout my childhood and adolescent years. It would, I thought, provide a helpful basis for my animation – a familiar form of expression through which I could explore motion and content. Susan Pitt's *Asparagus* was inspiring for yet another reason; it dealt with female issues, dreams and personal imagery and reinforced many of the ideas and feelings that I was experiencing at the time. I also found the films of Man Ray, Salvador Dali and Luis Buñuel compelling, but not to the extent that I was moved by Maya Deren's work. If you watch her films you can tell she's a dancer and that the message she conveys is distinctly female in character.

I took a dance class during my second year at Ohio State as a way of coming up with ideas for animation. It was a wonderful beginning choreography class and it helped me to connect the art concepts I had learned during my undergraduate studies to my dance roots. I made a series of exploratory dances that expressed raw feelings. I opened up emotionally and dealt with personal issues that began to manifest themselves in my approach to animation. It was during this period of discovery and after the complete frustration of my first year that I made the storyboard for *Broken Heart*. I finally felt that I had found my creative voice in the medium.

Q: Would you comment on the surrealistic imagery that you used in *Broken Heart* – the outsized stabbing forks, for example – and why the natural order and scale of familiar objects are so dramatically altered?

JS: Just a quick comment about audience responses to *Broken Heart* before I go into depth about the actual production of the film. It's been surprising to me to see the range of reactions that this work has produced when it's screened. For instance, when I showed *Broken Heart* to a women's mental health group at a Columbus, Ohio hospital nobody asked me what the animation was about. They knew that it was about an eating disorder; they understood the content. At the opposite end of the spectrum I've had people tell me that my work was too exhausting or too incomprehensible to view. Some people have told me that I wasn't a serious artist because my work didn't address traditional formal art concerns. I think when a film focuses on personal feelings and is about disturbing subject matter, people tend to have extreme and sometimes even conflicting reactions. This was certainly the case with *Broken Heart*. It's been a very controversial work.

While I was making *Broken Heart* I didn't tell anyone about the content of the piece because I was ashamed and embarrassed to discuss the core issue, which was my long fourteen-year struggle with anorexia and bulimia. By the time I was in graduate school I had recovered enough to have only intermittent problems. But it was still an unresolved issue and *Broken Heart* somehow became a way of dealing with this illness. However, I had no idea that creating this work would become a kind of catharsis for me and significantly contribute to my full recovery.

Some of the actual imagery in *Broken Heart* was derived from a poem I wrote during graduate school called "*Forks Against Porcelain*". On one level the poem was about tenderizing meat in my mother's kitchen, but on another level it was a metaphor for my eating disorder. The forks in *Broken Heart* are human in scale, emphasizing the power that the eating disorder had over my life. Text

All images: From *Broken Heart* (1988), by Joan Staveley.

from the poem was used in the sound track and consisted of phrases such as "stab-jabbing to break tough blooded, red meat". In the poem the meat being stabbed and wounded represented my body and the fork doing the stabbing signified my eating disorder. Forks were an important symbol in *Broken Heart* because, in addition to being associated with food and the eating disorder, their shape and physical function has a certain violent connotation. On the other hand,

forks are also seen as useful tools – symbols of gentility – that assist us in feeding ourselves. I see this as a metaphor for certain aspects of our culture. So often the practical and socially accepted instruments that we use also function as tools of viciousness and destruction.

To develop and "blue-print" the content of *Broken Heart*, I storyboarded, wrote poetry, painted, drew using a stream-of-consciousness approach, played

Right: From Wanting for Bridge (1991),
by Joan Staveley.

few fall from the sky. It was very important for me not to indicate explicitly why the birds were shot or to show who was shooting them. Many of the most important questions in life go unanswered and many of the important events and conditions that shape our lives are outside of our control. Scene four is a death scene that includes multiple views of dead birds raining from the sky. This "rain storm of death" eventually fades out followed by a fade-in to an outsized white hand with a stigmata torn into it. In the final scene it's morning. The "rain storm

of death" is over. The road has turned into a river of death and mourning. Dead hands float gently down the road below the broken bridge with the moaning sound of a female and whales in the background. Like the opening sequence of the film, part five is a close-up showing the same continuum of hands flowing next to the curb of the road, in effect, a reflection of our interminable human condition.

Wanting for Bridge, which is six minutes long, took roughly a year to complete. I did part of it while a grad student at Ohio State and finished it later,

working independently with my then partner graphics programmer Jeff Faust. Again, a number of friends and associates assisted with the production process. The Prix Ars Electronica[11] money I was awarded in 1989 for *Broken Heart* helped to fund the project and bring it to completion.

Q: **Your career has spanned more than a dozen years and involved a wide variety of projects. Specifically, what do you find most exciting or satisfying about computer animation as a medium of expression?**

JS: What I like most about computer animation is its potential for exploring the imagination and making up "plays" and "dances" in virtual three-dimensional space. I find it an incredibly absorbing and soothing type of work, notwithstanding the fact that there are moments when the technical aspects of the process are extremely difficult and frustrating. Another feature of computer animation that I find attractive is its collaborative possibilities. I like to work with other people and I want and need their input when I'm involved in a project. It's a working arrangement that draws on my experience with dance. For instance, if I'm the choreographer I work with my dancers to help them understand my concept and bring their own vision to the project. I approach my role as animation director in the same way. On the other hand, if I'm the dancer – as I was when animating the "money guy" for Chris Landreth's *Bingo* – I try to understand the choreographer's concept and to work as creatively as I can within those parameters.

Q: *Bingo* **(1997) is an extraordinary example of 3D animation both in terms of technique and content. How did you become involved in this project?**

Both images: From *Wanting for Bridge* (1991), by Joan Staveley.

JS: I first worked with Chris Landreth in 1995 while I was employed as an animator at Windlight Studio. Scott Dyer, the president of Windlight Studio offered to do the motion capture for Chris' animated film *The End*. Chris was working at Alias/Wavefront at the time. It was his job to create animations that, in effect, showed off Alias' new software techniques. Scott has always been a huge supporter of creative work and his gesture to assist Chris was a continuation of his interest in helping with innovative projects.

Because of my past work, mainly the art-oriented animation I did at Ohio State, Scott asked me if I wanted to work with Chris on motion capture. Chris and I knew of each other's work and I was thrilled to have an opportunity to collaborate with him. I lined up two dancer friends who I knew would be right for the project

Right: From *MEMB* (1993), a computer animated short by Robert Darroll.

evolution in its present state. It was with this idea in mind that I began to experiment with a pictorial form that consisted of a series of images depicting archetypal processes. I'm referring here to processes such as disintegration, evolution, attraction, repulsion and the changing hierarchical relationships of objects in space. These early works took the form of storyboards because, at the time, I didn't have access to the equipment that was needed to translate them into animated films. The pictorial elements that composed these images were seen as three-dimensional and could only have been convincingly animated with digital technology, which in the 1960s was beyond reach. When I arrived at the Art Academy in Hamburg in 1971, I was fortunate to meet Kurt Kranz, an instructor, who much earlier in the Bauhaus class of Kandinsky, had been working on similar themes. With the availability of adequate film equipment at the Academy and the support of Kurt Kranz, I was able to embark on my own animated experiments and explore for the first time the actual possibilities of time and motion.

Q: In 1972 you filmed Kurt Kranz's *Form Studies*, a series of sequential drawings that syntactically explored a variety of abstract themes and time-based strategies. Amazingly, these drawings were produced in the late 1920s and although they were never made into an actual motion picture by Kranz, to a certain extent they anticipated the development of abstract animation as an art form. How exactly did you get involved with this project and what kind of effect did Kranz's sequential drawings and this film project have on your own work with animation?

RD: After arriving in Hamburg I found that the animation equipment at the Academy had been sorely neglected and was not being used. I was the only student who, having gone off to work at a commercial studio to learn the operation of the rostrum camera, could actually use the Academy's animation equipment. So I was the ideal candidate to translate the designs that Kurt had produced at the Bauhaus in the 1930s and 40s into animated images. The original drawings, in fact, were not fully animated and I had to create in some instances the in-betweens and short cross-fades needed to maintain a sense of continuity. One thing that particularly impressed me about the project was the fact that Kurt had produced storyboards for colour film long before colour film was invented. It indicated an attitude, which for me was avant-garde in the very best sense. However, it should be pointed out that shortly before he created his first abstract storyboard *Schwarz/Weiss*, in the late 1930s, Viking Eggeling and Walter Ruttmann had already been working on the *Diagonal Symphony* and *Opus 1*. So I think it's fair to say that abstract animated film was "in the air" and that there

was a broad interest in it. The only reason so few examples actually emerged from this era is that it was an extremely expensive technique and with the arrival of the Depression, followed by the prohibitive artistic control of National Socialism, the opportunities for artists like Kurt Kranz to realise their projects were less than seldom.

Kurt Kranz was never really, in the strictest sense of the word, my teacher. Although I had a great deal of respect for him I thought of him as an older colleague. It was through our many casual conversations that I learnt a great deal from him, in particular the use of colour as a language in its own right, the dramaturgy and continuity of moving images and so on. Through him I was given the sense that I was working in the forefront of an experimental movement, but with a long tradition of Western visual art behind me.

Even though the tradition of abstract animation was not very old, I was able to see not only its relationship to contemporary painting and new music, but also its connection to the past. However, Kurt was a child of the Modern Era and I was unable to follow his unswerving conviction in a Formalism that was largely design oriented. I agreed with him that the formal aspects of a work must be of the highest possible standard, but also felt that there was more to making art than just design. Our approach to content constituted a gap that separated us – perhaps it was the already opening gap between the Modern and the Post-Modern movements. Kurt's sequential drawings called *The Heroic Arrow*, traces in a highly abstract manner, the course of an arrow through insurmountable obstacles, finally and unerringly reaching its target. It's an arrow that from my point of view reflected a highly questionable ideology. In the third part of my film, *Moe's Field*, I deliberately quoted *The Heroic Arrow*, but in this case the arrow is a hapless victim of circumstances, subjected to the vicissitudes of its environment and despite its strivings, freed of all Lyotardian "narrative" and orientation – an arrow without a point. Around this time I became involved with the writings of Max Bense, a German who was an authority on semiotics and a brilliant lecturer. His theories provided a certain comfortable sense of orientation, specifically a belief in the ability to analyse precisely all sensory data and almost statistically derive meaning from it. There was always a meaning – a statistical literal equivalent or analytical synonym – and it was as though one merely had logically to decode the data to find it. As a result, there was a tendency to think that using specific visual signs in specific ways would lead to specific meanings or effects. As Serialism in music proved to be a dull *cul de sac*, so too did its visual counterpart.

My attempts to integrate these systems into my creative work failed hopelessly and I produced what must have been some of the most boring rubbish of its time, which has fortunately long since seen the inside of the waste bin.

Q: Your visit to Korea in 1983 and your experiences in a monastery while you were there seemed to have had a profound effect on your consciousness and the direction of your work. After returning to Hamburg from Korea in 1984 you immediately began working on your *Korean Trilogy*, an animation project that would take you six years to complete. Would you discuss how this Asian experience manifested itself in your work and why it was such a powerful source of inspiration?

RD: After struggling with semiotics and the theories of Max Bense, I felt the need to re-examine what I was doing. What, for instance, was the point of making art and what kinds of questions should be addressed? How do I go about finding the answers and if I believe I have found some answers how do I formulate them into a visual language? This was part of the overweight luggage I took with me to Korea. Fortunately I have never found the answers to these questions, but rather I've constantly had to reconsider my position.

What I did recover in Korea was my intuitive ability to work creatively without putting the effect before the cause. Making art for me has become a parallel process, it's the formulation of a position directed in the first degree towards myself and in the second degree towards whoever wishes to look at my work. My point is that Korea allowed me to break through the shackles of formalism and analytical theory in order to regain access to an intuitive and spontaneous source of creativity. Making art became, as it had been earlier, a source of sensuous and intellectual pleasure as well as a satisfying quest for meaning.

Q: The three films, *Lung*, *Feng Huang* and *Stone Lion*, that form the *Korean Trilogy*, are basically composed of abstract animated imagery. How do you structure your abstract works? Do you use a storyboard for continuity or do you basically improvise as the work develops? In other words, do you use an in-process approach rather than executing a clearly orchestrated plan that is prepared before actual production begins?

RD: I have always prepared highly detailed storyboards for all of my projects. In recent years I have filled out the details less and less but a basic overall compositional arc is of essential importance. However, after having completed the designs I don't feel obliged to strictly adhere to these plans. There's little fun in simply executing a fixed storyboard. Therefore, during the production I take great liberty with my own ideas, but the work never becomes a purely in-process approach, which from my point of view tends to result in a random series of visual events. We perceive a film as an onward flowing "present moment", but our perception of that moment is unavoidably coloured by our memory of the past

Above: From *Moe's Field* (1997), by Robert Darroll. In this work Darroll employed conventional hand-drawn animation combined with video footage and computer animation. This hybrid technique was also used in other works that followed including *Stele*, *Noemata* and *Bedlam*.

**Q: Would you discuss your new installation project, *Bedlam*, and how it relates to the chrono-
logical development of your work with animation?**

RD: My work, over the years has gone through three phases of development,
starting with the three parts of the *Korean Trilogy*, which were all hand drawn,
cel-animation. From *Memb* to *Noemata No.2*, I continued exploring the possibilities of new digital technology, while remaining within the confines of the short
experimental film format. The iotaCenter in Los Angeles has just documented
these digital works together on one DVD.

Now, I am primarily interested in placing animation into a new context such
as installation or performance. In February and March of 2005, together with
Sean Reed, a composer originally from the U.S., I produced a 36 minute,
animation-installation for five synchronised large projections, at the (ZKM) Center
for Art and Media, in Karlsruhe, Germany. Entitled *Bedlam*, the installation
consisted of looped projections so that it could run over a longer period of time.
Technically, this work did not break new ground because we were primarily
interested in creating a strong, emotive statement. Our intentions were not to make
a merely attractively designed formalistic piece, nor did we attempt to fascinate
the viewer with technological acrobatics. The piece was aimed at moving the
viewer emotively, at confronting and challenging the viewer, nudging him or her
to reflect on what the work was saying, on their own act of perception – all acts
of perception – on an existential position in a brave new technological world –
mine, theirs – while considering the fact, that it is only a small percentage of
humanity that may enjoy the pleasures and horrors of this wonder, the rest are
too busy hunting for food and water. The work was based on a performance text,
which I wrote in 2000, for five performers. It consists of a dialogue for five voices.
Each voice was recorded and translated into an animated collage as well as a
tonal collage. There were three levels of media: recorded speech, animated
imagery and an electro-acoustic composition. The five screens were set in a bay
around the viewers, who were able to hear and see the pentalogue taking place
around them. I think that this animation-installation was strongly influenced by
my work with Japanese students. Perhaps I attempted to instill in them the idea
that revolutionary minds create revolutionary art, not revolutionary technology
alone and then, without noticing it, I was influenced by my own teaching.

Q: What sort of vision do you have for a technological art of the future?

RD: I find that to be an interesting but rather perplexing question. I can very well
envisage the possibility of vast holographic spaces in which we interact with
complex, poetic structures of form, colour and sound, unfettered by head-mounted
displays and cables:

The ultimate sensual, aesthetic illusion.

I can very well envisage a precise virtual imitation of the world in such a way
that the real world cannot be distinguished from the virtual world; a godlike
reconstruction of the world in an attempt to finally redesign, control and understand
it:

The intellectual illusion of illusion.

I can very well envisage wandering through surreal, dreamlike worlds in
which other physical laws operate and in which the time/space continuum is
illogically warped. In these worlds the meaning of things lies only in their tenuous,
connotative relationships, like the products of some deeply hidden substrata of
human consciousness:

The dream of ultimate intuition.

I can very well envisage a finely designed virtual space in which to vent all
pent up rage and violence in an exquisite choreography of mutilation, rape and
sexual excesses. A discrete and private space that is far beyond the borders of
human decency and in which a pinkly glowing sphere of high romantic love will
also beckon frustrated housewives and sweaty teenagers. An almost suffocating
illusion of excruciating emotion.

I suppose virtual spaces of one kind or another can be imagined that cover
all facets of the human mind and its expressive needs. However, if we do follow
these paths to their ultimate, radical conclusions and arrive at any clear insights
into the nature of our existence, we might well return to sit on some lichen covered
rock like our primordial ancestors and finally remain speechless.

Prologue to *Bedlam*

Below is the Prologue to *Bedlam*, an animation-installation produced by Robert
Darroll in association with composer Sean Reed. The work was based on a
performance text and consists of a dialogue for five voices. Darroll, who wrote the
text, comments as follows: "I include here, the Prologue to *Bedlam* in an effort to
simulate it's ambient textually. In fact, the Prologue is the program text for the
work."

* * *

All this, believe me, is quite senseless.

It is pure bloody Shambles. (I may be lying.)

Nevertheless, more attractive than dubious certainty, senselessness, a clumsy
bow-legged clutter of viperous sounds, drives that which may possibly distinguish
homo sapiens from the dull, four-legged plodders which he eats, at least until the

plodders too, learn to rise up on their hind quarters, and search the horizon, the sky, the Shambles for some speck of tenuous meaning gleaned from the distance between two objects, and then exclaim, in perfect Hindi, "that rock looks just like Madonna", or "those stars form the exact outline of a 1957 Studebaker Champion". All the while, the Shambles steadfastly remains the Shambles, as we passionately concoct it and tear it apart to make strawberry quarks and DNA and co-polymer latex from primordial bouillabaisse.

If there is one thing we do incessantly well, then it is to search for abstruse relationships in the Shambles. Large bodies collude in agreement, chorusing in frightful unison, "We shall prevail". Agreement again about the fact that the rock does not look like Madonna, or any Madonna, but rather like Queen Beatrix of Holland, as the Winter sun fell on her left cheek, while she wistfully contemplated a sliver of rapidly aging Gouda.

No, It was Edamer. Two slivers.

Ultimately, when we too return to the Shambles, when the 2nd Law of Thermodynamics (you know, the one about entropy) collides with the brilliantly ordered structure of DNA, we have the choice of three kinds of Hell, the Hell of Total Sense, the Hell of Total Senselessness, and the special, gruesome Hell, the contradictory, co-habitation of both of these, and, if we delve (and delve we will) into the mess, all that may remain at the very bottom of the barrel, will be a squat singularity filled with pointless monologues in a deaf and blind world (God, why did you not make it dumb too?) in which perfect Hindi is and always will be, incomprehensible.

And the "intentions"? Newton's clock ran down because it was clogged with matted swathes of "intentions", like the smelly stuff smugly nested in the U-bend of a toilet drain; you know its there but you can't see it. You deduce its presence from the rising tide approaching the rim of that porcelain world. "Ah! So there are intentions!", we exclaim perplexedly. But it is hopeless to intend in the face of Shambles. And yet we do, causing our own misery. It's our own fault. I told you so. You might as well, for lack of a cell phone, tap Morse on the bars of your cell window. Shakespeare did nothing else.

The Age of Information was constituted by nothing more (or less) than disparate squeaks and bleeps; all of them abandoned orphans searching for a kind mother's breast. ✧

Notes

1. Warner Bros. is known for the production of *Looney Tunes*, an ongoing series of animated shorts that featured characters such as Bugs Bunny, Daffy Duck, Tweetie Bird, Sylvester the Cat and Elmer Fudd, among others. Many of the Warner Bros. Cartoons were conceived and directed by animators Chuck Jones and Tex Avery.

2. During the 1970s, an interest in works by untrained artists (various kinds of Folk Art, for example) began to grow. Collectors of this work started to call the artists "outsiders" because they were outside of the main stream of the American art community. The term "outsider art" has also been used to describe works by contemporary artists that intentionally avoid the influence and limitations of established art movements.

3. Lumia, a term coined by light artist Thomas Wilfred (1888–1968), generally refers to artworks that use mobile light projections (usually in the form of light modulators) as a medium of expression.

4. Punk zines are underground comics that are characterized by their informal graphics, brash humor and subversive content.

5. Jacob Bronowski has written extensively about human evolution and the creative process. See "Jacob Bronowski: A Retrospective", *Leonardo*, Volume 8 Number 4, 1985.

6. See Cynthia Goodman, *Digital Visions* (New York: Harry N. Abrams, Inc., 1987), 116–117.

7. See Paul Heckbert, "Making the Magic Egg: A Personal Account", *IEEE Computer Graphics and Applications* (No. 6, 1986): 3–8.

8. The San Diego Supercomputer Center is a national center for supercomputing research. It provides a wide range of computing facilities and services for a consortium of universities and research centers around the world, including high-end 2- and 3-D graphics and animation in its Advanced Scientific Visualization Laboratory. It is located on the campus of the University of California at San Diego.

9. *Maya* was premiered in the "Perspectives Proximities Perceptions" exhibition at the Strong Museum in Rochester, New York, 11 July – 7 August 1993. Curated by Lance Speer, this show was part of Montage '93, the International Festival of the Image. The music for *Maya* was made by Rand Steiger with assistance from Tim Labor. It was generated with CSound running on a NeXT computer. Reverberation was later added using a Lexicon PCM70 processor. The score file was generated with a program that chooses randomly from among a range of harmonics, specified by the composer. The music was intended to reinforce the formal structure of the animation. Sections are differentiated by changes in fundamental frequency, rate, length and range of harmonics.

10. For more information about Sorensen's views about art and science, see Vibeke Sorensen, "Art, Science", *ACM SIGGRAPH Computer Graphics*, Vol. 29, Issue 4, November 1994).

11. Since 1979 Ars Electronica has been exploring issues at the nexus of art, technology and society. Located in Linz, Austria, Ars Electronica provides an annual venue for symposia, and electronically based exhibitions that include various forms of visualization, music and performance. It is the largest and oldest international festival of media art.

12. Founded in 1997, ZKM/Center for Art and Media is a unique cultural institution that has as its mission the integration of art and media. Located in Karlsruhe, Germany, the ZKM complex consists of two museums, the Institute for Acoustic Media, the Institute for Visual Media, the Mediathek and the Media Theater. The Institutes for Acoustic and Visual Media provide production facilities for artists, along with opportunities to experiment with new technologies and discuss future directions.

From written interviews, 2000 and 2005.

as *Particle Dreams* (1988) in which procedural techniques were used. Procedural animation is when a computer program determines the details of objects or motions instead of having them generated interactively by a person. Particle systems and plant growth simulations are both examples of this approach. When making *Panspermia,* I extended this idea by using interactive artificial evolution to "breed" specific botanical forms. The subject matter of the piece is also about a self-propagating system.

Q: Can you say what inspired the unusual theme of this animated work?

KS: I was interested in procedural modeling, including the automatic generation of virtual plants, and at the same time I was interested in self-propagating systems and artificial evolution. The subject matter of *Panspermia* – a life cycle of intergalactic botanical life forms – seemed appropriate for both demonstrating and creatively using those techniques.

Q: How long did it take you to produce *Panspermia*?

KS: Perhaps most of a year, but it's very hard to say because a lot of software had to be written from scratch for the project, including an entire 3D renderer for the Connection Machine CM2. I was also working on other things during that time.

Q: I understand that while producing *Panspermia* your decision-making process regarding the growth and evolution of forms was largely based on aesthetic criteria – the survival of the most aesthetically pleasing visuals. Would you discuss the basis for your aesthetic judgements?

KS: I was looking for any interesting 3D branching patterns, rather than having preconceived goals or applying any kind of formal aesthetic criteria. Basically, it was an intuitive process. I selected the virtual structures that I felt were the most visually satisfying and engaging.

Q: Who has influenced your work? Are there artists, animators or scientists whose ideas and work have in some way affected your creative production?

KS: I would say the greatest inspiration has been from nature itself. It's the most amazing "artist" of all in my opinion.

Below: From *Panspermia* (1990), by Karl Sims. In this computer animated work Sims used self-propagating systems to create a surreal world inhabited by an aggressively reproducing inter-galactic life form.
Right: From *Particle Dreams* (1988), by Karl Sims.

Q: Would you discuss the sexual content of your work with computer animation? I am referring here, of course, to the breeding, procreation and growth of digital organisms.

KS: For all my artificial evolution work, sexual recombination of virtual "genes" is just an option. It's not a requirement. In my installation *Galápagos* (1997), for example, when users only select one individual organism it will reproduce asexually using mutation alone for variation. Only if two are chosen at once do they mate and combine their "genes". So far it seems that interesting results still occur easily without recombination, although it can probably help in some cases.

Q: *Galápagos* is perhaps your most ambitious project to date. How would you describe this installation?

KS: *Galápagos* is an interactive Darwinian evolution of virtual "organisms". Twelve computers simulate the growth and behaviors of a population of abstract animated forms and display them on twelve screens placed on pedestals and arranged in an arc. Viewers select which organisms they find most aesthetically interesting by stepping on floor sensors in front of the exhibit's display screens. The selected

organisms survive, mate, mutate and reproduce. Those not selected are removed and their computers are inhabited by new offspring from the survivors. The offspring are copies and combinations of their parents, but their genes are altered by random mutations. When a mutation is favorable, meaning the new organism is more interesting than its ancestors, a viewer is more apt to select it. As this evolutionary cycle of reproduction and selection continues, more and more interesting organisms can emerge.

The evolving imagery of *Galápagos* is the result of a collaborative process between human and machine. Visitors to the installation provide the aesthetic information by selecting which animated forms are most interesting, and the computer provides the ability to simulate the genetics, growth and behavior of virtual "organisms". But the results can potentially surpass what either human or machine can produce alone. Although the aesthetics of the participants determine the results, they are not designing in the traditional sense. Rather, they are using selective breeding or individual mutation to explore the "hyperspace" of possible

Above: A gallery view of Karl Sims' *Galápagos* (1997), an interactive media installation that allows visitors to organically evolve 3D animated forms.

Left: From *Panspermia* (1990), by Karl Sims.

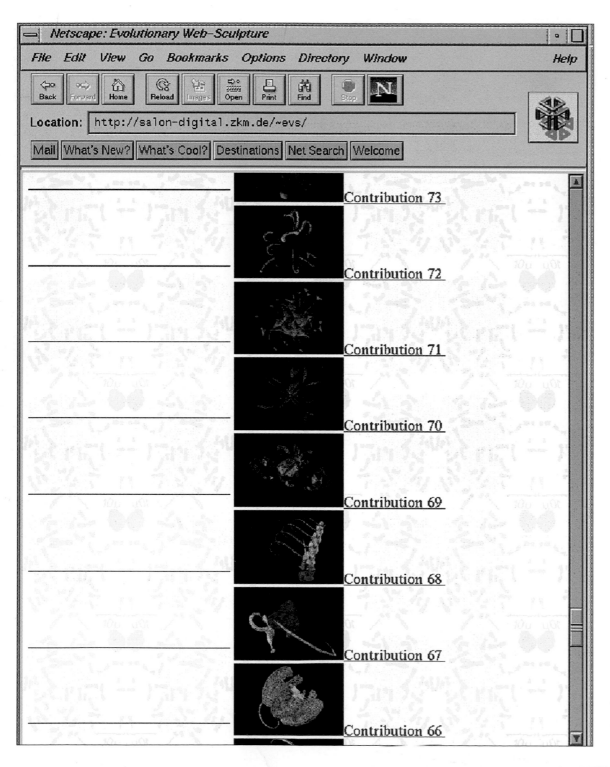

Interview with
BERND LINTERMANN

Q: You were educated as a computer scientist. How did you become involved in the art of animation?

Bernd Lintermann: Although my studies at the University of Karlsruhe (Germany) were in computer science, I've always had an interest in art and motion pictures. My mother is a photographer and an artist, and many of my friends are artists. Throughout most of my life I have been involved, in one way or another, with both art and computer science. When I attended the University of Karlsruhe I decided to combine my interests and to concentrate on the artistic possibilities of computer graphics. I had no interest, for example, in preparing for a career in developing databases and the like, but rather I wanted to focus on graphics and pursue my interests in programming and methods of visualization.

As a student I became particularly fascinated by the design characteristics of mandalas – their symmetry, proportions and reoccurring numerical structures – and I tried to figure out if it was possible to create a programming tool that was capable of generating variations of this form. I didn't want to redesign the entire form, but simply to input data about the essential characteristics of a mandala and then have the programming tool do the rest automatically. When I actually wrote the program for this procedure about five years ago (1994), there was no tool of this type available, at least none that I was aware of at the time. In any case, the development of this program was the starting point for the software that was later used in the production of several interactive works including a ZKM project entitled *conFIGURING the CAVE* (1997), Bill Viola's *The Tree of Knowledge* (1996–97) and *Morphogenesis* (1997), now revised and called *Sono-Morphis*.

I found that as my work with mandala forms progressed, I began to envisage other possibilities that led to changes in my original program. Instead of just using the characteristics of the mandala as a model, I began incorporating form principles observed in nature such as the golden section and the Fibonacci series. These principles opened up a new avenue of exploration and contributed to the development of certain kinds of genetic algorithms that, in turn, could be used to create and mutate three-dimensional organic objects. While working with these algorithms I discovered that it was more interesting to see these volumetric forms grow and change in real time, rather than to see individual still images of the process. As a result, I began to animate these organic shapes using stereoscopic recording techniques so that they could move and evolve in an illusory space. The elements of time and motion added a new and dynamic dimension to the imagery and became an integral part of the process. Ever since childhood I've been fascinated by the idea of making movies and I was delighted that these new kinetic and temporal possibilities had manifested themselves. At any rate, the software that was originally designed to create mandalas continued to developed and became an increasingly efficient tool for creating, complex animated displays of mutating organic imagery. One of the more interesting features of this software, which is called "Xfrog", is its real-time interactivity. For example, when the parameters of the procedural description of a model are changed during the programming process, the results are manifested immediately. This real-time interactive capability, when used in conjunction with the other features of "Xfrog", provides the basis for a very different kind of time-based visualization.

As a work is programmed using this real-time interactive approach, every procedure during a model's development is assigned different parameters and the way these parameters are combined determine how the model will look. For instance, when I develop an algorithm it's impossible for me to know in advance what will happen once these numerous and varied parameters are combined. As a result of this unpredictable process, I discovered possibilities that I never dreamed of. The imagery that resulted was quite fantastic and I soon began concentrating on interactively, exploring in real-time what the system had to offer. I felt it was far more satisfying to have immediate feedback while actually programming the images, rather than trying to conceptualize the outcome before hand.

It became apparent to me that this real-time interactive approach, if applied to artworks and installations, had the potential to provide a completely different viewing experience than the fixed linear time structure of a conventional motion picture film. When a film is viewed a second or third time, it's the same as the first screening, but when genetic algorithms are addressed using a real-time interactive approach, the imagery is never the same. It was this idea that led to the development of *Morphogenesis*. I wanted to create an installation work whose imagery had a fresh and unpredictable growth pattern. Each moment of the visual display, therefore, would take on a special importance because it would never be repeated. Its continuous and ever changing imagery would, in a sense, alter the role of the observer and have a different kind of psychic dimension. The form and content of *Morphogenesis*, which is idiomatic to the computer, is based on this type of procedural concept. It emphasizes the importance of the moment and the viewer's position in time, thereby creating a perceptual experience that's entirely different from conventional motion pictures.

Q: Would you describe what a viewer sees and experiences while interacting with *Morphogenesis*?

BL: Basically, *Morphogenesis* is about the evolutionary development of three-dimensional organic form. By using a control panel, a visitor to the installation can change and shape the dynamic behavior of life-like organic objects in stereoscopic space, producing a continuous and endless variety of mutating visual effects. During this process, formal patterns that have been extracted from the natural world are combined arbitrarily by the software, generating graphic creations that appear familiar, but in fact, have never before been seen. The evolving organic imagery could be described as an abstract and synthetic manifestation of various structural principles found in nature.

Above: Stream (1998) by Bernd Lintermann, a still picture of a landscape composed of various types of plant forms that were individually generated with genetic algorithms.

Facing page: Web interface for *Sono-Morphis*. Lintermann's and Belschner's interactive installation can be addressed from two coupled access points: a gallery installation and the internet. Actions on the web affect the installation and *vice versa*. The online interface extends the work's accessibility and creates a broader and interconnected audience.

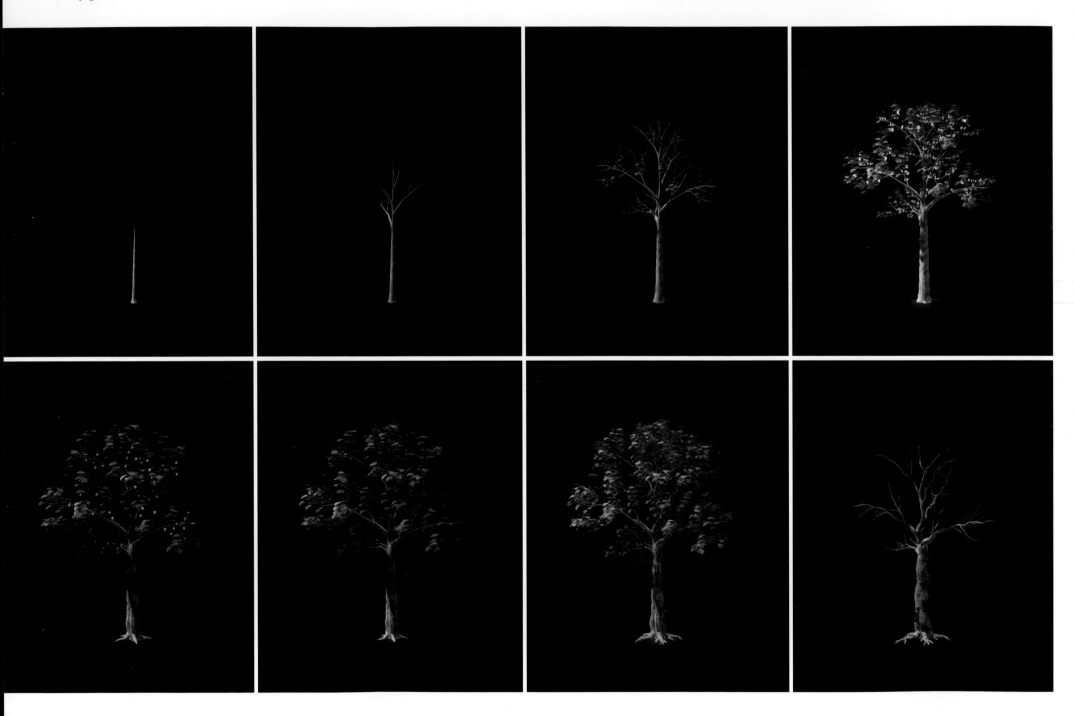

Above: A sequence from *The Tree of Knowledge* by Bill Viola. The organic software used to animate the growth and transformation of the tree form for this interactive installation was developed by Bernd Lintermann.

Recently, *Morphogenesis* has been extended by sound and renamed *SonoMorphis*. In this new version, there is a direct correlation between the sound genes and the visual genes of the piece. As a result of this linkage, the sound along with the organic objects can be simultaneously mutated and transformed by the user. The sound was produced by Torsten Belschner, a composer and research fellow here at the ZKM.

Regarding its actual display and distribution features, *SonoMorphis* can be addressed from two coupled access points. One of these access points exists in real space as a gallery installation where visitors, via a control panel, interact with virtual organic objects that are displayed on a large projection screen. The second access point uses the World Wide Web as its user interface. The two systems are coupled and operate using the same data set. Actions on the web affect the gallery installation and vice versa. Therefore, if a change on the web happens, the organic objects displayed in the gallery installation slowly morph toward the web selection. On the other hand, if the installation's imagery is changed it directly affects the next web action. The basic idea is to extend the work's accessibility and to create a wider and interconnected audience by putting *SonoMorphis* online.

Q: In addition to your own work you have also programmed imagery for other artists. For example, in 1996–97 you assisted Bill Viola in the production of his interactive installation, *The Tree of Knowledge*. How would you describe this work?

BL: The imagery for *The Tree of Knowledge* is composed entirely of three-dimensional computer animation. Viola's concept for the piece involves a virtual tree that algorithmically evolves through all its developmental stages and seasonal changes. He selected arboreal features from numerous photographs and then described to me how the tree should look and transform itself. I then employed customized software that simulates growth processes such as forking and branching, and that results in a form of animation that is entirely computer generated, yet natural looking.

A viewer experiencing Viola's installation enters a corridor, just wide enough for one person, and confronts a computer-generated tree at larger than human scale. At entry, the image of the tree is a sapling, but as the viewer advances toward the projection each step along the way affects the ageing process of the tree. A laser scanner is used to trigger the changes and any perceptible motion of the body results in a recognizable transformation of the image. The viewer can thereby age the tree or rejuvenate it by moving back and forth in the corridor. In *The Tree of Knowledge* the tree is designed to exhibit all the seasonal markers that so richly symbolize the various stages of life. Its interactive features allow the

viewer to incrementally control time and to contemplate through this process the nature of change and evolution.

Q: Did you employ your software, "xfrog", to produce the visual transformations in *The Tree of Knowledge*?

BL: Yes, but unlike *SonoMorphis* the openness of the system was not used. It was a different type of application.

Bill Viola wanted the tree form in the installation to be a composite rather than a specific tree like an oak, for example. In other words, he wanted the tree to appear natural, but at the same time seem unfamiliar. So a decision was made not to use the openness of the system, which could generate many different kinds of trees, but instead to create a single generic tree that could grow and evolve naturalistically. In effect, it was a narrow and specialized application of "Xfrog".

Viola's idea was to use this computer-generated tree as a metaphor for a human being. To achieve this, the tree's transformation and changing seasons were designed to suggest different phases of the human life cycle. We weren't concerned with describing the characteristics of a specific tree or with producing various mutations of different trees, but rather with using a symbolic tree form to make a statement about the organic and temporal natured of human existence.

Viola wanted each change in the development of the tree to remind the viewer of some stage of the human life cycle. We started the project by making a simple time line from birth to death and plotted the changes and corresponding characteristics that occur with age. For example, at the end of one's life one tends to slow down and eventually become inactive. The roots of the computer-generated tree, at this point, grow out and become more pronounced. Old age also causes a person's posture to change and often the spine develops a certain curvature. This type of deterioration, along with other physical changes brought on by the ageing process is also reflected in the final stage of the tree's evolution. The installation, then, was designed and programmed so that there would be an analogous relationship between every stage of the tree's growth and the span of a human's lifetime.

Overall, the project was a rather complex programming assignment. In order to meet the specific conceptual requirements of the installation I had to make certain revisions and adjustments during the programming process. However, by conforming "Xfrog" to the needs of the Viola project, the software demonstrated its versatility and also suggested new possibilities for future artworks and installations. ✧

From an audiotape interview, 1999.

Interview with
TORSTEN BELSCHNER

Q: As a musician and composer, what exactly attracted you to the computer?

Torsten Belschner: It was discovering the tremendous amount control that could be achieved with digital techniques. When I was a youngster, a friend of mine who had a computer and media sequencer showed me how he could control the various properties of sound, something that I was striving to achieve at the time as an aspiring instrumentalist. With a simple movement of the mouse he could draw a curve and configure over a hundred different sound events. I was amazed that sound output could be defined and manipulated so precisely and with such ease. It soon became obvious to me that the mouse had certain limitations and that much more could be done by creating customized programs; in effect, digital control data that could be used to produce complex musical structures. The computer and its unique capabilities opened up a world of new and exciting opportunities for me. It provided a fresh range of technical and expressive qualities that are not possible with conventional methods of composition and production.

Q: You recently teamed with Bernd Lintermann, a computer programmer and visual artist, to produce an installation work called *SonoMorphis* (1998). How would you describe *SonoMorphis* and what was your role in this project?

TB: *SonoMorphis* is an interactive stereoscopic display of virtual 3D organic objects. A computer simulates the growth and behaviors of these abstract animated objects and displays them in an illusory space. Sound is an integral part of the computer program and is designed to correspond to the visual activity. By wearing stereo spectacles and using a control panel placed in front of the display screen, a user can participate in creating the imagery and sound of the installation by selecting virtual objects and organically transforming them. The selected objects can be made to move, change size and evolve, producing random mutations and simulating the genetics and behaviors of virtual organisms. As these visual transformations are created, they trigger parallel changes in the sound structure. Bernd programmed the graphics for the installation, basically using genetic algorithms, and I produced the computer-generated sound component.

Q: Would you agree that the sounds of *SonoMorphis* have a very synthetic quality and that, at times, they even have metallic or machine-like characteristics?

TB: Yes, that was my intention. I wanted to create an interactive sound structure that exploited the unique audio-generating capabilities of the computer. I was not interested in replicating traditional musical instruments or even electronic music, but rather I wanted to produce qualities and effects that were integral to the machine. In order to do this, it's important to understand the inner workings of the machine, all the way down to the hardware level, and to explore the kinds of sounds that are idiomatic to its architecture. My aim, then, was to produce sounds for *SonoMorphis* that remain linked to their origins and that had properties that were clearly the product of a technological medium.

Q: The sound, as well as the stereoscopic imagery of *SonoMorphis*, has a real dimension of depth. Would you discuss the dynamic quality of the installation's audio-space and how its sounds relate to the 3D objects within the visual space?

TB: Essentially, the spatial location of the sounds corresponds to the spatial location of the objects. By using the controls on the interface panel the objects, and therefore the sounds, can be moved in all directions. For example, if an object is moved forward, and as a result increases in size, its corresponding sound will move with it and increase in volume. The spatial audio effects come from four speakers, one in each corner of the room. The balance of the sound coming from the speakers is calculated according to the location of each object in the stereoscopic space. As users become familiar with the installation's interface, they can explore its many interactive features and discover ways to orchestrate the evolution of virtual objects and their related sounds.

Right: Torsten Belschner.

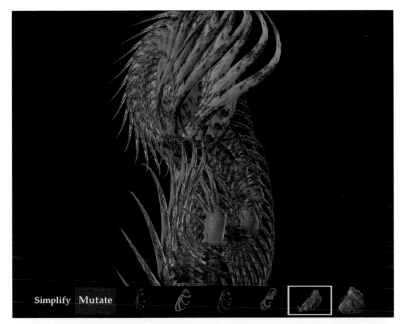

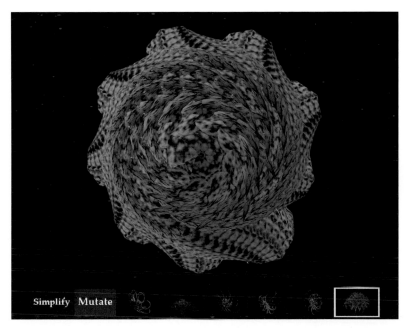

Above: From *SonoMorphis* (1998), by Bernd Lintermann and Torsten Belschner.

fact, had been exhibited publicly in 1997. An administrator, here at ZKM, who thought I might be interested in Bernd's work with computer graphics, sent me several still pictures of his abstract organic imagery. I was impressed by the pictures, overwhelmed really, because they conveyed the impression of incredible complexity and also because they were the product of what was apparently a very sophisticated digital imaging system. I immediately e-mailed Bernd and expressed my interest in his work. Although we were both in residence at ZKM, I didn't known him at the time; in fact, I didn't know then that the pictures I had seen were individual still frames taken from animated imagery. I was under the impression that Bernd was using an imaging system that only produced still pictures. Later, I met with Bernd and he explained that he was working with animation and he showed me the 3D stereoscopic version of the project. I was, of course, very excited by what I saw and my immediate response was to suggest that the imagery needed sound. Bernd liked the idea so we began developing an audio component for the installation, which took us about a year to complete.

Q: When you compose music, is it a completely abstract process, essentially concerned with formal issues, or do you have some kind of theme or subject matter in mind?

Q: Were you involved with *SonoMorphis* from the beginning, or did Bernd contact you at some point after he had started the project?

TB: When I first became aware of Bernd's work he had already finished the image world of what was later to become *SonoMorphis*. It was completely done and, in

TB: It's different from either of those approaches. For instance, when I hear sounds, even random or arbitrary sounds, I see the sounds as forms and imagine them to have certain shapes, colors and surface textures. On the other hand, when

Jon McCormack

A signal artist of the digital generation, Australian animator and media specialist Jon McCormack develops his moving life-like imagery primarily by writing computer software. Using an interdisciplinary approach to form and content that fuses art, science and technology, he has produced an extraordinary body of work in a wide variety of display formats, ranging from interactive laserdisc and stereoscopy to DVD and high definition television.

After receiving a BS degree in applied mathematics and computer science from Monash University, Australia, in 1986, McCormack continued his education at the Swinburne Film and Television School where he majored in animation. He then worked for several years in commercial computer animation production before pursuing his own projects. As his work with digital imaging developed, he became increasingly involved with the examination and interpretation of natural systems through the formulation of genetic algorithms. Notable among his animated shorts are *Flux* (1992), *TISEA Animation* (1992) and *Technillusions* (1993).

During the early 1990s McCormack also turned to interactive installations as a form of expression. His laserdisc installation, *Turbulence*, which premiered in 1994, is considered a defining work in the field of media art, winning awards and securing numerous international exhibitions. A project that took over three years to complete, *Turbulence* is a kinetic array of synthesized forms evolved with the computer through a process of artificial selection. The heart of the installation is a video laserdisc that contains thirty minutes of state-of-the-art computer generated animation. The laserdisc is accessed via a touch-screen interface, allowing visitors to the installation to interact with a collection of poems, information and organic animated imagery relating to the philosophical impact of evolution on contemporary thought. Visually and conceptually engaging, *Turbulence* is lyrical, informed by tech-culture, and offers a new perspective on nature and our relationship to it.

Since 1987 McCormack has exhibited at many Australian and international venues including the National Gallery of Victoria, Australia; Ars Electronica, Austria; Siggraph, USA; Centre Georges Pompidou, France and the Museum of Modern Art, USA. In addition to his own animated shorts and installations, McCormack has participated in collaborative projects with animators, media

artists and writers. He is currently a lecturer in computer science at Monash University, Melbourne.

Interview with JON McCORMACK

Q: Would you begin this interview by discussing your education and background and why you turned to computer animation as a form of expression.

Jon McCormack: I have always enjoyed math but never really understood the point of it until one day, while in college, I wrote and executed a simple program for the interactive exploration of multivariate equations. It was a crude program, but my understanding of what was going on was much greater than if I had just written the equations or graphed them on paper. From that point I realized that the computer was an incredible machine for enhancing one's understanding of a system or idea, particularly when used in the "heuristic" mode.[5] The dynamic and interactive nature of digital technology and its capacity for revealing and manipulating process was unlike anything I had ever experienced before.

Following my math and computer science studies I enrolled at the Swinburne Film School (Australia) where I majored in animation. I've always had an interest in the cinema and I've made films ever since I was a child. I also had a background in photography, a medium whose experimental possibilities and darkroom processes fascinated me as much as the aesthetics of the photograph itself.

At film school we had several computer systems that were used for animation including devices such as the Fairlight CVI, for example. The equipment was relatively simple when compared to current technology: however, from the moment I first used these machines to produce animation, I knew that the computer was going to be the medium I wanted to work with. I was particularly impressed by its capacity for synthesis and for composing in time and space using logical processes. It had the potential, I felt, to be a rich and deeply meaningful domain for investigation.

Also contributing to my interest in digital technology is the fact that ever since my days as a maths student I've been fascinated by the idea of "computational

Facing page: From *Turbulence* (1995), a virtual museum of un-natural history produced by Jon McCormack. In this participatory installation piece digital simulations, electronically evolved forms, text messages and poetry are all part of a multiplex of links into an interactive web of synthesized visuals.

Above and facing page: From *The Morphogenesis Series* (2000–2005), by Jon McCormack. Based on a personal interpretation of natural phenomena, this collection of computer synthesized still images explores the growth and development of plant-like structures and their aesthetic possibilities. Their intensely delineated detail suggests "otherworldliness" and at the same time a believable reality that might exist in an unknown place.

have very little knowledge and struggle to survive. However, over time, some learn to find solutions that will keep them alive a little longer than the others of their generation and thus their learning system is rewarded. Eventually the successful creatures may mate and produce offspring who inherit what the parents have learned throughout their lifetime (this process is a kind of Lamarckian evolution).

The thing that makes *Eden* interesting is that the growth of biomass in the virtual environment is affected by (amongst other things) the presence and interest of people in the physical installation space. The creatures have no direct knowledge of this, but they do require an abundance of biomass to stay alive, and hence to pass their digital 'genes' to the next generation.

The creatures have the ability to move, eat and fight. They can also make sounds, a characteristic that, in a very significant way, affects their survival. For example, in the virtual world they can use sound as a defence mechanism, as a way to ward off predators. In addition to being heard in the virtual realm, the sounds that the creatures make are *sonified* and thus heard by people in the installation space. Infrared sensors located near the screens detect the presence and movement of people viewing the installation. Their presence provides nutrients in the virtual world near where they are standing, causing food to grow in that area. Now if the creatures make interesting sounds, they will tend to attract and hold people's interest. Consequently, the food supply for the creatures increases, giving them a better chance of survival. In some instances the creatures learn that by singing, they can get more food. Of course they don't know why this happens because any activity that takes place in the physical space is outside of their experience. Nevertheless, these populations are implicitly rewarded by the presence of people listening to them and as a result a symbiotic relationship develops between the real and artificial worlds.

Q: Would you describe the physical layout of the installation? What exactly do people see and hear when they visit *Eden*?

JM: Physically, the work consists of two large intersecting translucent screens (about 3m x 4m in size) that are configured in an 'X' shape when viewed in plan. Two video projectors are used to display the computer-generated imagery in real-time. Because the projection surfaces are made of translucent material, images can be viewed on both sides of the screens. The visual shapes that compose the world look like changing abstract cellular patterns; however when studied for a while the work's formal organic process begins to become apparent. The piece was originally conceived and inspired after I'd visited Litchfield National Park, a wilderness area in the Northern Territory of Australia. The patterns that

interactive and directly connected to the environment's non-representational imagery. Would you discuss the form of this work and how sound came to play such an important part in its development?

JM: *Eden* is a kind of 'toy universe' with very simplistic representations of a physical world and only three basic types of matter: rocks (immovable obstacles that break up the environment), biomass (a food source that grows) and evolving virtual creatures. The creatures have a machine learning system, which allows them to adapt to their environment. This learning mechanism helps prepare them for activities such as finding food, defending against predators, avoiding rocks – bumping into them hurts – and so on. At the start of the simulation, creatures the artificial world makes, although not any kind of literal representation, reminds me of some of the things I experienced during that trip, such as the sight of termites crawling over sandstone rocks in the park, or the design of the landscape viewed from the air.

The physical layout of the installation, its configuration of screens and speakers, was designed to function as an integrated experience, an immersive interactive environment that blurs the boundary between the real and the virtual spaces. To augment this idea, the installation uses a fog machine that gives the projected images a wonderful atmospheric quality. The experience is like walking through a three-dimensional space made of light – a kind of 'phantom space' that's populated by electronic simulacra. Several sets of speakers are used to spatially position audio effects within the installation. As a result the sounds that a particular creature makes can be heard coming from the general area that the creature inhabits.

Q: Would you discuss how visitors interacted with the piece? In other words, how did they cause evolutionary changes in the work and to what extent were visitors aware of their participation? Also, what kind of ideas and feelings do you think were generated by the installation?

JM: *Eden* is part of a series of on-going experiments into what I call 'reactive' environments. In many interactive computer environments there are very direct and limited causal relationships between an action and that action's effect on the simulation. This comes from the commercial and industrial origins of computer simulations and environments, where clear and direct causal relationships are the norm (e.g. in the user-interface metaphors of buttons and sliders). Artists tend to devise more exotic and interesting interfaces, but most of these still require that you learn their 'language of interactivity' in order to engage the work. In a traditional gallery setting, this can create a problematic situation for the viewer. With reactive environments such as *Eden*, there's no interactive language to learn. You just experience the work, and through your experience you change the work. So the experience is like one of being in a limited natural environment, not in terms of the sensory information, but in terms of the types of interaction you might experience. In *Eden* visitors don't need to know that the creatures are evolving or that their presence is growing food for them, although after some time they might be able to appreciate what's actually happening. In this sense the interaction with the work is very much a phenomenological experience. For instance, some people have told me the installation reminded them of being in a forest at dawn. Others I think 'understood' the work as a unique aesthetic experience that didn't require a rational explanation of how to interact with it because that kind of action-reaction

mode of engagement just isn't necessary in a work like *Eden*. What I think most people appreciate about the piece is that it's provocative and stimulating and tends to engender a new sense of nature and the natural. *Eden* offers a different mode of engagement with technology, one that doesn't emphasize purpose and function so strongly, but rather attempts to offer a broader phenomenological understanding of natural systems, even though there is clearly nothing 'natural' about it.

Q: The digital process of breeding and formalizing artificial life is now available to the artist and animator as a new and radically different approach to creative expression. What kind of effect do you think this new techno-scientific development will have on the art world at large? Will it essentially remain a parallel and specialized creative activity, or will it in the future have a significant impact on the way artworks are produced, exhibited and experienced?

JM: I think many of the ideas from artificial life as well as from chaos theory, non-linear systems and so on, have already entered the popular imagination, albeit in a highly distorted way. For the immediate future, I think advanced forms of visualization will be an accepted, but marginalized area of endeavor in the same

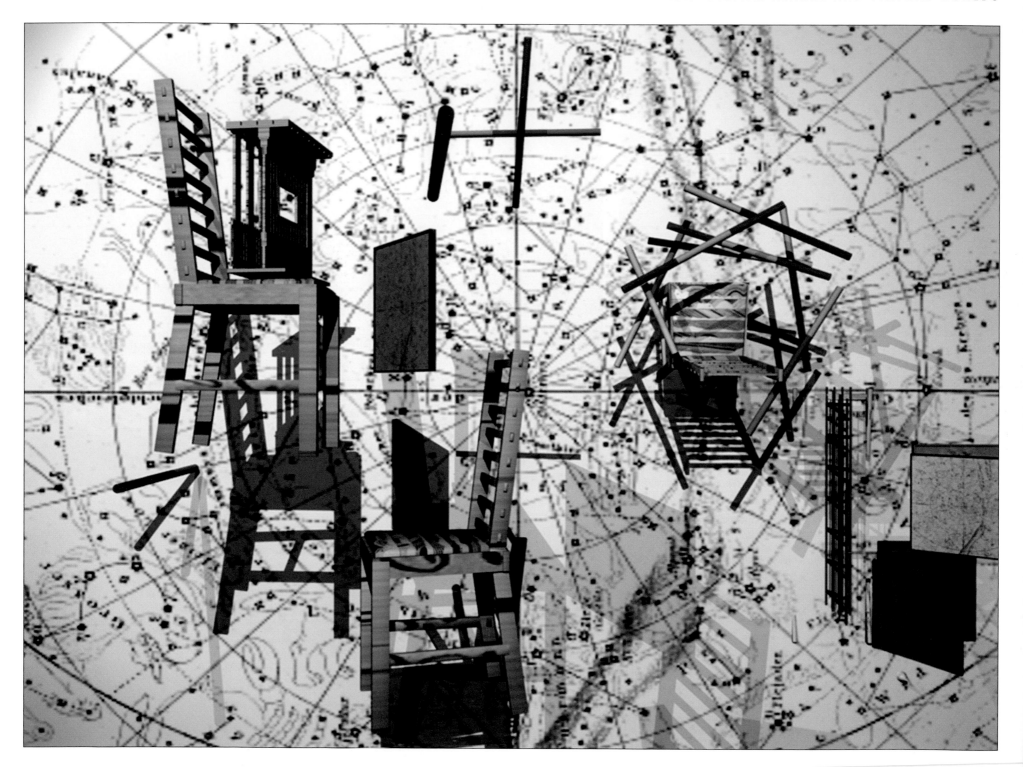

4 Interactive and projection installations

One of the most productive and prominent developments in the field of Hyperanimation falls within the purview of digitally based installation art. These high tech event spaces, which employ advanced forms of motion graphics, represent an astonishingly diverse sphere of ideological viewpoints, stylistic currents and aesthetic interpretations. Subject matter includes figurative and non-figurative imagery, sometimes within the same work, and a spectrum of ideas that range from social and technological topics to biographical and metaphysical issues. Artists working with interactive and projection installations are posing new questions, many of which have grown out of the development of imaging technology itself, but also arise from a transformation of aesthetic issues and a renewal of attitudes about the nature and definition of art. As a result, digital media have not only fundamentally changed the formal context of the moving image and animation, but have opened up a new avenue of experimentation and altered the role of cinema as a vehicle for artistic expression. Whether it is by engineering interactive displays, or creating imaging systems that involve multiple screens and non-linear projections,[1] installations as a form of Hyperanimation have been an effective vehicle for the production of artistic experiences that are not possible in the television and motion picture industries.

We make our instruments, and then they make us, changing our perceptions, our image of ourselves.
– Heinz Pagels

Image has become architecture, a space to visit, to explore in various ways.
– Frank Popper

Although the essential features of today's installation projects have a long history and can be traced back to environmental works of other periods, for example, the artistically embellished architectural spaces of the Baroque era, its more recent and direct antecedents consist of participatory forms of expression that developed after 1960. Happenings, Fluxus intermedia events, as well as film and video installations all helped to prepare the technical and conceptual foundation for the digital works that began to emerge in the 1980s. This second wave of installations, which exists at the intersection of art, techno-science and computer mediated communications, has introduced new strategies and formats that significantly changed the aesthetic profile of the genre. Today's artists who use Hyperanimation in an installation context no longer consider the image as a standard projection, but rather as a complex means of imaging that can be configured in physical architectural space and digitally manipulated and re-formatted in a variety of ways.

In this chapter, two kinds of digital installations are discussed: interactive works and non-linear multiple screen projections. In the category that involves interactivity Jeffrey Shaw, Agnes Hegedüs and John Klima are representative of a growing number of artists who have produced pieces that allow the viewer, through various kinds of interfaces, to create their own psychological spaces.

These interactive installations attribute a role to the spectator that is unlike the type of participation that takes place when viewing traditional time-based art forms. A person viewing a theatrical motion picture, for example, interacts with the film, but in a strictly internalized way. The main difference, therefore, is that in the case of cinema the participation of the spectator does not change the motion picture itself, whereas in computer-based interactive art, the viewer's interactivity can actually modify the work and its evolutionary development. Interactive art offers the possibility of intervention and provides opportunities for the viewer to make aesthetic judgements and, in a sense, to complete the piece. Although the final outcome is unpredictable, the work is still a product of the artist's concept and not something entirely different. By creating a program and endowing it with a rational impulse for development, it is the artist (or team of artists) that is responsible for the core design of the installation and for the interpretive dialogue that ultimately takes shape.

A good example of this process can be found in the sophisticated interactivity of Jeffrey Shaw's *The Legible City* (1989–1997). In this work, the viewer sits on a stationary bicycle in front of a large projection screen, using the handlebar and pedals to "ride" through a simulated representation of a city that is graphically

Facing page: From *Red Fence* (1999), a multi-screen animation-installation by Paul Glabicki.

mass media, involve the spectator in a protean plastic display that has a different kind of spatio-temporal dimension.

The digital projection installations of Paul Glabicki are indicative of this new type of multi-screen presentation and certainly must be considered among some of the most visually complex hyperanimated works produced. Glabicki, who achieved an international reputation with hand-drawn animated films such as *Five Improvisations* (1978) and *Under the Sea* (1989), turned to 3D computer animation and installation work during the mid-1990s. Designed to be exhibited in a gallery context, rather than a conventional theater, his configurations of large-scale multiple screen projections such as *Dark Room/Simple Roof* (1998), *Red Fence* (1999) and *Full Moon* (2001) are composed of representational collage imagery that has been processed, re-structured and invested with new meaning. One of the few artists in the field of Hyperanimation that works unassisted, Glabicki is responsible for all aspects of the production process, from concept and animation, to editing and sound design. He has sought out fresh technical approaches and has continually added new programs and hardware to his computer image-making capability, often using it in inventive ways not intended by their makers. His installations, which are highly personal and beautifully crafted, emanate from his own observations, imagination and sensibility, free from the narrative and verbal conventions of mainstream film and television. In *Red Fence*, for example, the imagery consists of a series of sequences or "acts" that take place within a graphically rendered stage space, in effect, a theatrical performance of ever-changing objects and environments. In this piece, Glabicki is concerned with a re-occurring theme, the notion of "East" and "West" as distinct cultural entities and as sources for opposition and dialogue. Captivated by the symbols, architecture and landscape of foreign cultures, Glabicki animated his sequences, imprinting them with fragments of memory that recaptured his travels to Europe and the Far East. A red fence appears in every sequence and serves as a metaphor for the demarcation between "East" and "West" and as a device for directing and enhancing the viewing process. Sometimes the fence is a barrier, separating the spectator from visual information, while at other times it is used to focus attention on certain objects and structures. The imagery, which consists of digitally scanned collage material, was taken from a variety of sources including photographs, travel postcards, old maps and illustrations. The accompanying sound track, like the imagery, is a collage and was composed of diverse audio segments, ranging from ambient effects and the spoken word, to chants and classical musical fragments. When *Red Fence* is displayed as an installation piece, it is projected continuously onto screens placed at various locations within a gallery space. Although the same animated imagery is used for each screen it is shown randomly and out of sync, thereby creating complex juxtapositions when seen by visitors as they walk throughout the installation. Glabicki's multi-screen presentations reflect the way he thinks, sees and feels as mediated by digital technology. The logic and rigorous discipline of the computer and its software are confronted by his intuition, creativity and a sense of personal vision. Within this dialogue of art and technology, Glabicki has found the means to subvert and rearrange reason, expand the parameters of animation, and provide insights into cultural diversity, memory and the complexity of human experience.

When digital technology is used in conjunction with installation art, form and content are continually redefined from one work to another or even in the frame of a single work. With interactive and multi-screen projections, the spectator and the environment participate in this redefinition, leading to a different kind of experience than one encounters in the mass culture discourse or even in the traditional arts. The so-called artificial world of images and the real world of physical space do not oppose each other in these new digital works, but rather are closely interconnected areas. Dealing with this type of experience challenges the viewer and requires a sensibility that has to be partly re-learned and partly found anew. However, it is only through lively curiosity and a willingness to experiment that the unexpected appears and leads to the asking of different questions.

Jeffrey Shaw

A pioneer in the field of media art, Jeffrey Shaw has been creating seminal interactive installations for more than thirty years. Throughout his career he has, on the one hand, been concerned with expanding the artistic and technical dimensions of the moving image, while at the same time allowing the viewer to actually influence its form and content. It is a conceptual theme that can be traced from the large inflatable objects that served as environments for film projections and audience participation in the late 1960s, to the interactive computer generated imagery of the 1980s and 1990s, through to his most recent multisensory telematic pieces.

One of Shaw's best known works, which has been shown in both Europe and America, is *The Legible City* (1998), a participatory installation that allows viewers to explore the terrain of a virtual urban environment, a simulated representation of a city constituted by huge computer-generated 3D words and sentences. Other works that have been shown widely include *The Virtual Museum* (1991), *The Golden Calf* (1995), *Place-a user's manual* (1995) and *Web of Life* (2002).

Born in Australia in 1944, Shaw studied architecture and art history at the University of Melbourne. He continued his education at the Academia di Belli Arti di Brera in Milan then went on to do postgraduate studies in sculpture at St. Martin's School of Art in London. Following graduation, he lived in Amsterdam where he co-founded the Eventstructure Research Group and held several teaching positions. In 1991 he was appointed director of the Institute of Visual Media at the Center for Art and Media (ZKM), Karlsruhe, Germany. Currently, he is co-director of the Center for Interactive Cinema Research (Icinema) at the University of New South Wales, Sydney, Australia. Shaw has received numerous grants and awards including L'Immagine Electronica, Ferrara, Italy and the Prix Ars Electronica, Linz, Austria. His works have been exhibited at international venues such as the Centre Georges Pompidou, France; Siggraph, USA; Hara Arc Museum, Japan; the Fine Arts Museum, Taiwan and the Guggenheim Museum SoHo, USA.

Interview with JEFFREY SHAW

Q: Would you begin this interview by discussing the chronology of your early work and how you became involved with digital media?

Jeffrey Shaw: In 1965 I left Australia to attend the Academia di Belli Art di Brera in Milan, Italy, but after studying for about a year, I found making paintings and sculpture somehow difficult and problematic. I moved to London and shortly after arriving there I had my first contact with what was then the tail end of the Fluxus movement.[2] There was a big symposium at the Institute for Contemporary Art called *Destruction in Art Symposium*, where I saw the work of both European and American Fluxus artists. The work was fresh and innovative and had a healthy disregard, not only for traditional art disciplines, but for high modernism as well. Overall, I was very impressed by the exhibition and in particular with the performance and participatory events.

Almost immediately, I shifted from mainly making sculpture to doing performances and installation art. I started using pneumatic structures in my work – large-scale air-inflated plastic forms – and produced a series of open-air multimedia events. At that time, there was considerable interest in the use of pneumatic structures in architecture and I became fascinated with these forms because they were relatively inexpensive, easy to construct and provided a responsive environment for audience participation.

Parallel to the production of my installation and performance works, I also developed an interest in cinema as a medium and made my first film with a Dutch associate, Tjebbe van Tijen. It was an animated work called *Continuous Sound and Image Moments* (1966) and it was generated from thousands of hand-made abstract drawings that were recorded frame by frame. Producing this film provided me with a fresh alternative to the problem of making a painting or a drawing, in

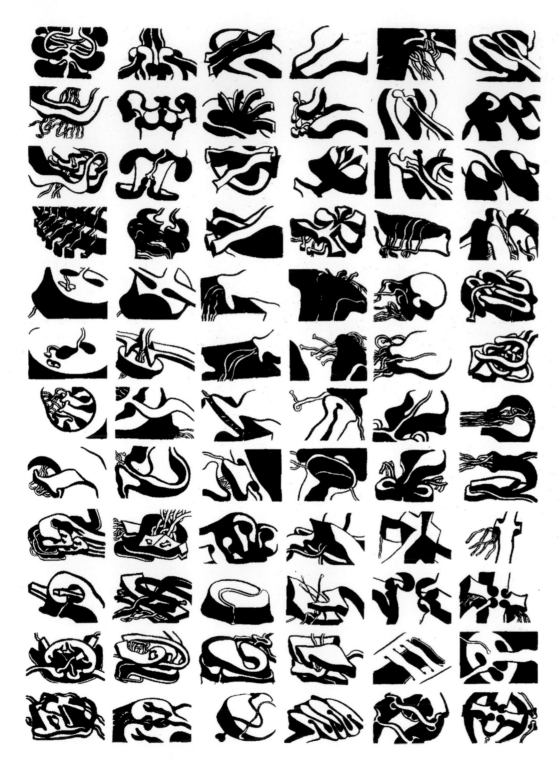

the same way that pneumatic structures provided me with a solution to the problem of making sculpture. By using film I was able to depart from traditional methods of picture making and focus on the temporal and kinetic process of creating images. Rather than making one drawing or a single painting, I found that film could extend and transform still pictures, creating a dynamic form of imagery that had the dimensions of time and motion.

Although *Continuous Sound and Image Moments* was produced using the technique of animation, we departed from the conventional single-frame process and used an entirely different approach for achieving visual continuity. Tjebbe van Tijen and I made thousands of abstract drawings for the film and recorded each of these drawings for only one or two frames. The result, unlike traditional forms of animation, was a rapid but coherent impression of images that was displayed at the threshold of perception. Our film was made into a loop so that it could be shown continuously with no beginning and no end. It was meant to be seen as an installation work and not as a film presentation in the conventional sense.

Q: Were your drawings for *Continuous Sound and Image Moments* a series of graduated images or was each drawing completely different?

JS: They were graduated, but not with the same kind of continuity that is used in traditional animation. Basically, the process consisted of Tjebbe van Tijen and me making alternating drawings. First, I would make an abstract drawing, and then he would pick up certain formal elements from my drawing and incorporate them into his drawing. My next drawing would adopt some of his formal elements, and so on. It was like having a conversation. Although the work involved a spontaneous exchange of ideas and responses between the two of us, it was quite apparent when the finished work was projected that there was a logical process involved in generating the imagery. As a perceptual experience, it was a very abstract and frenetic film, but if the loop was watched a few times it became evident that there was an internal development and a sequential progression of forms.

I used *Continuous Sound and Image Moments* for several years in an expanded cinema[3] context, projecting it along with slides and other effects, onto inflatable forms during performances. While I was involved with producing these large-scale events that used pneumatic structures and projected images, I started to spend some time in Amsterdam where I found a more receptive environment for my work. In the late 1960s after commuting back and forth to England, I moved to Amsterdam and almost immediately benefited from official Dutch Ministry of Culture support for my installation and performance projects. There was considerable interest in new art forms there at the time and, in general, I found the situation conducive to the kind of works I wanted to produce.

Q: Would you discuss the works you produced during your years in Amsterdam?

JS: Shortly after I resettled in Amsterdam, I formed a partnership with two other artists, Theo Botschuijver and Sean Wellesley-Miller, and together we formed an organization called the Eventstructure Research Group (1967–80). Our activities were essentially a continuation of the work I had been doing previously and mainly focused on developing outsized pneumatic structures that were used in conjunction with various kinds of multimedia performance. There were two events produced by the group that I think were particularly important and which incidentally incorporated *Continuous Sound and Image Moments* along with other kinds of projected effects. One was *Corpocinema* (1967), performed in Amsterdam, and the other one was *MovieMovie* (1967), created for the 4th Experimental Film Festival, Knokke-Le-Zoute, in Belgium. Both of these works were concerned with creating an expanded form of cinema, in effect, a three-dimensional experience that was immersive and interactive.

In *Corpocinema* we achieved three-dimensionality by projecting images onto a large transparent inflatable sphere filled with various substances such as smoke, confetti and fire extinguisher foam. These substances served to materialize the film projection within the three-dimensional space defined by the sphere. This sphere was designed so performers, along with the general public, could enter the space, freely interact with the film, and become part of the imagery. The notion of public participation was articulated even more dramatically in *MovieMovie*. In this event the inflatable structure was not spherical, but rather cone-shaped with an outer transparent membrane and an inner white surface that served as the floor of the piece. The imagery, which was projected from above, first impinged lightly on the tightly inflated outer envelope and then appeared on the semi-inflated inner white surface. The space between the transparent membrane and the white surface was where all the interactivity took place. People visiting the installation could actually jump onto the screen and into the movie. They could physically manipulate the soft surfaces of the structure and participate in the event by distorting and transforming the projected imagery.

My interest in interactivity, which began in these early events such as *Corpocinema* and *MovieMovie*, has continued over the years and since the early 1980s has been an important part of my work with digital media. For example, recent virtual reality projects, such as *The Legible City* (1989–97) and *conFIGURING the CAVE* (1997), have also used immersive tactics and are designed to

bring the viewer into the image and to encourage audience participation. So, in this sense, a certain coherent pattern of interactivity has evolved, an approach that allows the artwork to be transformed and recreated by the decisions and behavior of the viewer.

Q: For approximately the past twenty years you have used digital media as a means of expression. Specifically, what attracted you to the computer?

JS: Two things attracted me. One, of course, was the computers interactive capability. I saw this demonstrated for the first time during the late 1970s at a Siggraph conference. There was a computer screen that displayed a wire-frame

Upper image: Corpocinema (1967), an expanded cinema environment produced by Jeffrey Shaw. Presented in a series of open-air performances in Rotterdam and Amsterdam, the basic structure of the piece was a large air-inflated transparent dome onto which films and slides were projected.

Lower image: MovieMovie (1967), a multimedia performance produced by Jeffrey Shaw for the 4th Experimental Film Festival in Knokke-le-Zoute, Belgium. The intention of this work was to transform the conventional flat cinema screen into a three-dimensional kinetic and architectonic space for visualization. The inflated structure used for the piece allowed multiple film projections to materialize in layers while the bodies of performers and members of the audience (many of whom spontaneously participated in the nude) became part of the immersive cinematic spectacle.

Facing page: Still frames from *Continuous Sound and Image Moments* (1966), a hand-drawn black and white animated film made by Jeffrey Shaw in association with Tjebbe van Tijen. Conceived as a loop that could be projected continuously, the film was used in conjunction with many of Shaw's multimedia performances including *Corpocinema* (1967) and *MovieMovie* (1967).

Both images: From *The Legible City* (1989–97), an interactive installation by Jeffrey Shaw. In this piece visitors to the installation can ride a stationary bicycle through a simulated city in which outsized three-dimensional words and sentences form both sides of the street. Three separate variations of the work were produced using the actual ground plans of Manhattan, Amsterdam and Karlsruhe (Germany). The existing architecture of these cities was completely replaced by a new architecture of monumental text written and compiled by Dirk Groeneveld.

Another aspect of the computer that attracted me concerned the advantages of using software. I found that software freed me from my struggle with the type of large-scale physical structures and complex electromechanical devices that I had used in my early projects. When I became involved with the computer, I reduced my dependency on various kinds of materials and hardware that were difficult to manage, and with the help of programmers concentrated on the development of software applications. I realized that the computer and its programming capability could contribute to more efficient working methods while at the same time opening up an expanded range of artistic possibilities. I found, for example, that certain software tools could be recycled and then built upon from one work to the next. This developmental process has been an important strategy for me and I have used it in the production of all my digital work, beginning back in the early 1980s.

Q: *The Legible City* is one of your best-known works. How would you describe this interactive installation?

JS: I should begin by saying that I have produced several versions of *The Legible City* since 1989 and that this work has undergone a number of conceptual and technical changes over time. In the early versions of *The Legible City*, for example, the content varied but the technical configuration and display system was basically the same. A person visiting the installation would sit on a stationary bicycle facing a large video projection screen. By peddling and steering the bicycle this person would activate the imagery on the screen and, in effect, travel through a virtual environment, a simulated representation of a city constructed of letters. These

object, and this object could be moved and rotated by using a joystick as a computer interface. It was a simple form of interactivity; however, for me it was a new and radical experience. I had been brought up with television and the cinema, and the imagery I was accustomed to watching was always completely separate from my space as a viewer. After seeing the demonstration I realized that it was possible for the viewer actually to control the image on a screen with the use of a computer. I was very impressed and felt that it was a revolutionary development with immense implications for the way art is produced and experienced.

Jeffrey Shaw

letters, which appear monumental in scale, form words and sentences along the sides of the streets. The architecture of each city block, then, was transformed into a readable message. The literary content of the installation varies depending on which version of *The Legible City* is being displayed. The early variations of *The Legible City* include an Amsterdam version, a Karlsruhe (Germany) version, and the Manhattan version.

Q: The early versions of *The Legible City* involved digital and robotic features as well as considerable architectural research. How does someone go about putting a project together that has that degree of complexity?

JS: Regarding the practical side of producing *The Legible City*, I worked with three associates who are specialists. Gideon May was the computer programmer for the project and Dirk Groeneveld was the writer. I also worked with an engineer who helped design the electromechanical interface for the bicycle. It was the late 1980s and many of the things we were trying to do were relatively new and required original solutions. For example, one of the most difficult aspects of the project involved creating appropriate software tools that would facilitate our work. We were using a first generation Silicon Graphics computer and Gideon had never written code for this particular machine's environment. As a result, it took us quite some time to develop the software that we needed.

A large part of our work for the project involved creating a user interface, in effect, a set of software tools that would make it easy for Dirk and me to enter text into a database. Once this was accomplished, we implemented the first step in the process that basically consisted of digitizing the ground plan. For the first installation, the Manhattan version, we did this by simply digitizing a street map of Manhattan. Gideon then created a list that showed the names of all the streets and their respective lengths. The software he created allowed us to type in the text, the words and sentences we had written for each street, and to assign specific properties to each letter. In other words, we could indicate, in meters, the actual dimensions of each letter, its height, width and depth. We could also assign color to each letter. After these parameters were specified, the program allowed us to stretch or squeeze the text so that our written material would proportionally fit the length of each city block. Gideon's software took all of the information we entered into the computer and converted it into a 3D database. And then there it was – a fully operational virtual environment.

As far as the bicycle is concerned, it was simply an electromechanical engineering problem. We designed an interface that would output a continuous stream of data about the bicyclist's peddling speed and handle bar rotation. When

Both images: An installation view of *The Distributed Legible City* (1999) a networked multi-user work by Jeffrey Shaw. In this adaptation of *The Legible City* (1989–97), participants in remote locations are able to meet and talk to each other as they navigate a shared virtual space.

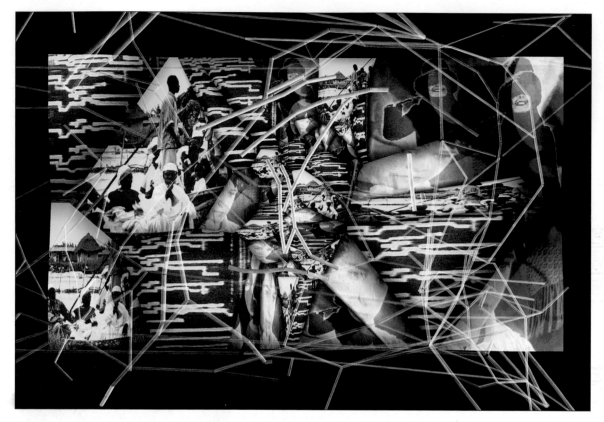

Above: From *Web of Life* (2002), by Jeffrey Shaw and a team of ZKM associates.

equipped with a head-mounted display, is immersed in the environment, other people can view the monitors and have some sense of what is going on.

Q: *The Distributed Legible City*, along with your other digital projects, has been produced in cooperation with technicians and other types of specialists. In general, do you find that the artworks being created today with complex technologies usually require some form of collaboration?

JS: I know some artists who have the abilities to produce this type of artwork entirely by themselves. They do their own programming, their own sound, and they build their own imagery. But generally speaking, media projects that employ new and multifaceted technologies usually involve collaboration. Many of the artists I know in this field work with programmers and depend on the engineering skills and expertise of other people.

Q: Do you feel, then, that the role of the artist is undergoing significant changes? For example, is the use of technology changing our view of creativity and our notion of the artist as genius?

JS: Yes, and it is not just technology that is causing these changes but a shift in the way we make and perceive artworks. What we now consider to be the role and practice of an artist is historically a fairly recent cultural phenomenon. For example, artisans who worked on gothic cathedrals or who produced the images and monuments of ancient Egypt were not thought of as self-expressing individuals, but rather as skilled people who were part of a collaborative process that was wholly integrated into the culture. There were no signatures on their works. Their identity and social function were quite different than in more recent times, and certainly in contrast to the modern art movement of the twentieth century. However, beginning in the 1960s and continuing through postmodernism, the role of the artist as well as the audience began to change. For instance, I see the artist as becoming more socially engaged and I also see the artist as inviting the viewer to become more engaged and more connected to the creative process.

Today, the authorship of a digital work can take many forms and operate on many levels. The artist can share authorship with other artists and with the viewer or user of the work. This open-ended process can even be extended to a point where the artist creates a "frame" and invites the viewer to use specially designed digital tools to make the work. I find this range of participatory and interactive possibilities a significant departure from the approach in which the artist acts as a single individual in total control of the creative process. It provides a fresh basis for new forms of collaboration and dialogue. We're now able to converse in new ways, using the immateriality of digital technology to speak to each other with images, sounds, words and movement.

Q: According to Arthur C. Clarke,[4] science and artificial intelligence makes significant advances about every five years and if we could look at what was happening ten years from now, it would seem like some form of magic. Given the evolutionary pattern of computers and their capability for dealing with multidimensional and multisensory issues, how do you view the future relative to your own work and the development of new media in general?

JS: Recently, I produced a work with my wife Agnes Hegedüs along with artist and computer scientist Bernd Lintermann, called *conFIGURING the CAVE* (1997). We used a virtual reality technology for the piece that was developed by Dan Sandin (chapter 6) and his team at the University of Illinois' Electronic Visualization Laboratory. It's called the CAVE and it basically consists of interactive stereoscopic projections on the three walls and floor of a room-like space. As a virtual environment, the CAVE has incredible illusionistic power. Compared to what these technologies were capable of just a few years ago, it offers an almost magical tool of representation and visualization. However, notwithstanding the remarkable capability of the CAVE, one should bear in mind that there are many artistic precedents for exploring the power and expressive possibilities of illusionistic space.

Looking back to baroque churches and the baroque theater, for example, one sees an extremely seductive combination of rich imagery and complex visual architecture. This type of multidimensional and multisensory approach to expression has occurred throughout the whole tradition of Western art. It has been used to captivate the viewer and create provocative and overwhelming experiences. Right now the CAVE is an up-to-date technology and a powerful visual tool; however, I imagine that ten years from now there will be other devices that are more advanced and they will provide a different and perhaps expanded range of creative options. What these new forms of visualization will mean for art in terms of imagery and content, however, is yet another question. Because media is evolving and becoming more immersive and convincing doesn't necessarily mean that there will automatically be better art as a result. Art, unlike technological media, does not evolve. There is no such thing as the evolution of art. Art addresses the issues of its time and sometimes those issues are timeless and that is when art goes beyond its time. But generally, artists communicate with their contemporaries and operate within a coexistent cultural context.

I know that five years from now I will continue to be stimulated and challenged by the possibilities of entirely new media and I look forward to the kinds of works I will be able to produce. But the prospect of more powerful and responsive equipment in no way diminishes my enthusiasm for the work I am doing at the moment and for the machines and materials I'm using now. Although we are currently undergoing a revolution of new forms and techniques, the exploration and articulation of human experience remain the essential domain of artistic research and production. In my view, the real challenge today is to focus on our immediate needs and resources and to instill meaning in those media that are an integral part of our current culture.

From an audiotape interview, June 2000.

Web of Life

Below is a synopsis of *Web of Life*, a networked installation produced by Jeffrey Shaw in association with Michael Gleich, Lawrence Wallen, Bernd Lintermann and Torsten Belschner. The synopsis appeared in a catalog that was published in conjunction with *intermedium 2*, a 2002 art exhibition at the Center for Art and Media (ZKM), Karlshure, Germany.

The installation at the ZKM in Karlsruhe is built around a large screen (3m x 8m) on which four high-resolution video projectors present a dynamic flow of three-dimensional images viewable by visitors with the aid of special stereoscopic glasses. Computed in real time, this projected imagery is continually creating manifold structures and patterns that evoke a dramatic network of pictorial and thematic relations such as neuronal circuits of the human brain, the leads on a printed circuit board, the urban lattice of streets, or the filigree of arteries in the human body.

The installation room is also fitted with a grid of more than 70 speakers distributed over the walls and ceiling. This enables the artwork's specially composed multi-channel sound composition to create a spatial web of three-dimensional acoustical experiences interactively and synergetically linked to the visual manifestation. This algorithmic tapestry of audiovisual and thematic correspondences is activated and modulated by the patterns derived from the palms of visitors' hands that have been scanned and entered into the system from the local and remote input terminals. These varied and always uniquely individual palm lines then merge into and activate a singular sequence of transformations on the screen as well as in the musical score that accompanies the imagery. In this way each visitor logs into and breathes new life into this immersive networked artwork; with a ritual handshake of solidarity they awaken a fascinating world of visual and thematic correlations and make themselves an important part of the *Web of Life*.

While one hand-scanning terminal accompanies the installation at ZKM in Karlsruhe, the four other specially designed terminals will travel to various locations throughout the world during the project's three-year duration ... Connected via the Internet both to the *Web of Life* installation at the ZKM and the *Web of Life* website these remote input terminals also have video screens and sound systems that provide the visitors with a "telepresent" experience of the audiovisual occurrences at the ZKM. ✧

Credits:
General concept: Jeffrey Shaw, Michael Gleich.
Projected imagery concept: Bernd Lintermann.
Projected video concept: Lawrence Wallen.
Audio concept and sound design: Torsten Belschner.
ZKM installation architecture concept and design: Manfred Wolff-Plottegg and Arne Böhm.
User interface concept and design: Michael Gleich, Jeffrey Shaw, Bernd Lintermann.
Produced at the ZKM Institute for Visual Media.

John Klima

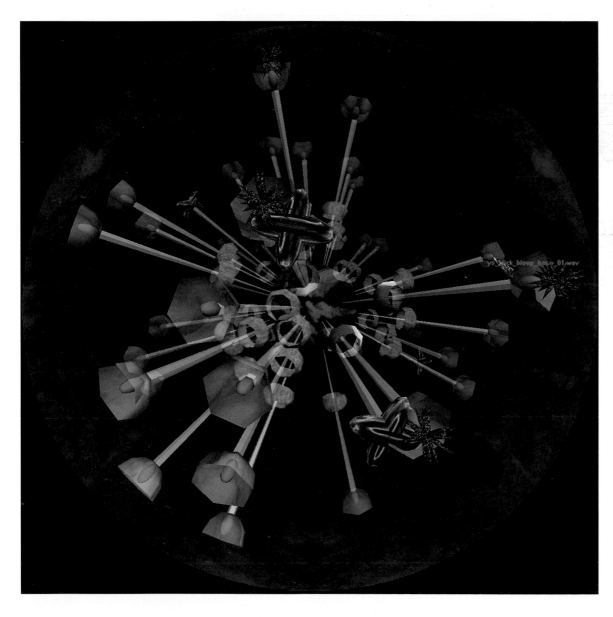

Using digital technology, telecommunications and computer programming, John Klima has developed interactive methods of visualization that have enhanced viewer participation and opened up new imaging possibilities in the field of media art. For instance, in a work entitled *glasbead* (1999), Klima produced a multi-user environment that enabled online players to create collaborative musical experiences by manipulating an elegantly designed visual interface. In another interactive piece, a wall-sized projection called *ecosystm* (2000), streaming weather and stock market data from the internet are used to control the kinetic activity and atmospheric conditions of a surreal world. Viewers participating in this installation navigate through an imaginary terrain, which is vast in space, using a hand-held interface device. Influenced by a life long interest in the strategies and technology of gaming, Klima's work blurs the distinction between art and entertainment and in a very profound way connects the virtual to the real.

Born in 1965, Klima began programming his own video games at age fifteen. He attended the State University of New York at Purchase and in 1987 earned a BFA degree in photography. Following graduation he worked for art galleries in New York for two years before traveling around the country, eventually settling in Seattle, Washington, where his interest in computers was rekindled. Within a year he was working for Microsoft as a programmer, writing code for customized computer applications. Klima returned to New York where he continued to work as a computer specialist while making art within the flexible schedule that freelance programming provided. In 1998 he discontinued activities as a commercial programmer to focus solely on the creation of art software.

Klima has shown frequently in New York, mounting his first solo exhibition in 2001 at Postmaster's Gallery. His work has been shown in Europe at venues such as the VIPER International Festival of Film, Video and New Media in Switzerland, and VRML-ART, a media festival in Germany. His work *glasbead* was included in the New Media New Faces exhibition at the InterCommunication Center in Tokyo and received the Golden Lasso Award for Art in the Web3D RoundUP at Siggraph 2000 in New Orleans. In 2001, *ecosystm*, a work commissioned by Zurich Capital Markets, was shown at the Whitney Museum

Interview with JOHN KLIMA

Q: After receiving a BFA in photography in 1987 and then moving about the country for few years, you began working as a freelance computer programmer for Microsoft and other companies. What events or circumstances lead you to leave the field of commercial programming and turn to making digital art works?

John Klima: After college I lived in New York City for a few years and worked as an art gallery assistant; however, I soon became disillusioned with what was happening in the art world and decided to leave New York. I didn't like any of the work that was being promoted at the time and on top of that I was finding it really difficult to make a living. For a few years I traveled around the country, first to New Orleans, then on to Chicago and Seattle. I was building art furniture for a living and began using a computer to do the design work. As it turned out, I grew more interested in the computer and less interested in designing furniture. Back in 1978 I had taught myself how to program on a TRS-80 – an early Radio Shack computer – and I sort of picked up where I left off, rapidly finding work in Seattle during the PC explosion of the late 1980s and early 90s. I quickly realized that with this line of work I could move back to New York, live well, take taxis everywhere, and dine out at expensive restaurants. After relocating to New York it wasn't long before I was making a lot of money and only working part time. It was then that I began to seriously explore the possibilities of programming as an art form. I soon discovered that people were actually interested in the work that I was doing and in a relatively short period of time I began exhibiting in major shows here in New York and around the world. I quit my part time job as a programmer and devoted myself exclusively to artwork.

Q: *glasbead* (1999), a web based interface, is one of your best-known works. Would you discuss the participatory component of *glasbead* and how it allows players to interact with its various audio and visual features? For example, how do players create sounds using the visual interface and, specifically, how do they adjust the sound's pitch, volume and so forth?

JK: When accessed on the web, *glasbead* allows a player to manipulate a 3D visual structure that in turn creates complex sequences of sound. The structure consists of two basic components. I call them "hammers" and "bells". Six hammers and 32 bells radiate from a central core. The player assigns sample sound files to the bells and then, using a visual computer interface, flings the bells and hammers around the core. When a hammer strikes a bell, it plays a sound. The central core can also be flung, creating asynchronous rotations that result in a non-repetitive looping and layering of sounds. Any sound files can be loaded into a *glasbead* bell effortlessly and on the fly. Players can also adjust the pitch and volume of the individual sounds by rotating a ring at the base of the bell. The goal was to create a work that was non-repetitive, easy to use and very flexible, a piece that would engage the player and allow him or her to "compose" by interactively assembling related sound files. Audio environments have been orchestrated for *glasbead* by a wide variety of people with different levels of skill, ranging from the uninitiated to several professional musicians who, at my request, composed distinct sets of sounds for the piece. The character of the sound that *glasbead* produces is completely dependent on the samples used and how it is played. It can be rhythmic, melodic or ambient, depending on the samples and how the interface is manipulated.

It should also be noted that *glasbead* has a multi-user capability. As many as 20 people can simultaneously play glasbead from remote locations around the world and all these players can see and hear the same thing. Sound samples are automatically transferred from player to player. If someone in Tokyo loads a file into a bell, it finds its way to a player in New York. *glasbead* is also "persistent", meaning that when a new player logs onto *glasbead*, that player begins where a previous player logged off.

Q: Does the work's title, *glasbead*, have some special significance?

JK: After completing *glasbead*, I realized that what I had done was akin to the game Hermann Hesse described in his 1943 novel *Das Glasperlenspiel* (The Glass Bead Game), or *Magister Ludi* as it's called in this country. Hesse describes the glass bead game as a futuristic activity, developing out of musicology and mathematics and capable of expressing a symphony of ideas and feelings. The game is more or less left up to the reader's imagination with a few hints at sources and influences, but with no explanation of how it really works. I felt that Hesse's imaginary game – an artistic concept really – was in many ways analogous to my web-based piece.

Another connection was the fact that Hesse has a bad reputation among some critics in this country for being the writer of choice among hormonally exuberant young men. I saw this kind of negative criticism as being relevant to

Facing page: A screen shot from *glasbead* (1999) by John Klima. This online multi-user musical instrument and its specially designed interface offer players an opportunity to create a wide variety of soundscapes.

a professor of art at the University of Pittsburgh, he has been a visiting artist and lecturer at institutions throughout the United States, Europe and Japan.

Interview with PAUL GLABICKI

Q: For a period of about twenty years you produced a prodigious corpus of hand-drawn animated films such as *Diagram Film* (1977), *Five Improvisations* (1978) and *Under the Sea* (1989). However, your more recent works, beginning with *Computer Animation Studies I–IV* (1990–93), were created with computer technology. Why did you begin using the computer as a form of expression?

Paul Glabicki: A turning point in my work came in 1989 just after I completed what was to be my last hand-drawn 16mm film, *Under the Sea*. That film was an ambitious four-year project that required more detailed drawing for each animation cell than anything I had previously attempted. In fact, I tried to make each drawing – representing 1/24th of a second of screen time – a unique work of art that could be viewed and appreciated on its own terms. As I reached completion of this project, I realized that it was a summary of everything I had done in film over a twenty-year period. On a practical level, each of my films was demanding more and more years of work. The volume of drawing and pictorial detail had reached a point where some new kind of tool was needed, something that could do more than I could do by hand. The computer, I felt, was a logical choice even though animation software at the time was primitive and I had absolutely no equipment or practical experience. I began looking into the possibility of using digital media and gained access to the engineering school's computer lab at the University of Pittsburgh where I teach. While at the lab I was introduced to PANDA, an early paint software developed by Harry Holland who was a self-taught programmer and painting instructor at Carnegie Mellon University. By today's standards the software was rudimentary, but it was easy to use and it helped break down the inhibitions I had about working with a computer. For about a year or so I produced an outpouring of digital drawings that were either displayed on a monitor or recorded onto 35mm slides.

In 1990, I received a research grant from the University of Pittsburgh that provided me with an Amiga 2000 computer and a NewTek VideoToaster. Included in the package were Digi-Paint and Deluxe Paint, two programs that were more sophisticated than those I had been using. After creating still images with Digi-Paint for a couple of years, I began exploring the possibilities of animation using Deluxe Paint. I was easily able to apply my previous film animation skills,

Pieces such as *Dark Room/Simple Roof* (1998), *Red Fence* (1999) and *Full Moon* (2001) are visually characterized by complex layered effects that fluidly combine both abstract and figurative imagery. Firmly rooted in the tradition of Experimental Animation, Glabicki's installations are composed of richly delineated cultural fragments; they are, in effect, mobile collages of imagery and sound that expand conventional notions of time, memory and perception.

Born in 1951, Glabicki studied visual art at Carnegie Mellon University before receiving two consecutive MFA degrees in painting and film at the University of Ohio. His media works have been shown at major venues such as the New York Film Festival at Lincoln Center, the Cannes Film Festival, the Museum of Modern Art and the Whitney Museum in New York, the Venice Biennale and the Hirschorn Museum in Washington, DC. The recipient of numerous citations and film festival prizes, Glabicki has been awarded fellowships from the American Film Institute, the National Endowment for the Arts and the Guggenheim Foundation. Presently

while being able to develop techniques I couldn't possibly create by hand. Over a three year period I produced a series of silent animation tapes, entitled *Computer Animation Studies I–IV*. Each tape was a 60-minute collection of animation cycles, a string of "motion paintings" that explored a variety of techniques ranging from multiple overlays and cut and paste animation, to simulations of 3D modeling. I became completely absorbed in the process. I had the feeling that I was somehow imprinting my imagination onto the medium while forming a kind of dialogue with the software and hardware designers who made it all possible.

The *Computer Animation Studies* were exhibited on either Amiga computers or video monitors. The largest and most ambitious exhibition of these works was curated by William Judson and shown in late 1991 at the Carnegie Museum of Art in Pittsburgh. Bill had curated numerous screenings of my film work at the Carnegie and he made frequent visits to my studio to observe my early computer animation work. He was interested in the form and content of the imagery I was developing, but somewhat alarmed that I was discarding and deleting so much of it. Because of limited computer storage space, week-old work would be rapidly replaced by new and stronger pieces. It was his concept to curate a multimedia exhibition that included the ongoing process of my animation, along with works I had done in other media. The exhibition consisted of three Amiga 2000 computers running animation loops that were created during the show and changed on a daily basis. The show also included two large video monitors displaying two different 60-minute tapes of *Computer Animation Studies*. Large drawings, photographs and other works from my studio were displayed on the walls of the gallery. The installation was designed so that it completely surrounded the viewer. I felt that the show was not only an overview of what I had done since my last film, *Under the Sea*, but also a clear indication that a significant artistic transformation had taken place in my work. It was an exhibition that shifted my focus from filmmaking and painting to installation work and electronic multimedia.

Q: Would you discuss the development of your installation work and why you were attracted to this art form?

PG: My first installation piece was part of a one-man multimedia show at the Carnegie Mellon University Art Gallery in 1990. It basically consisted of a diagrammatic wall drawing that was applied to a large recessed wall area at the rear of the gallery space. The drawing, which related to the imagery of my animated films, diagrammed the wall space with linear patterns and fragments of text. Because of this piece, I received an invitation to do a major project at Pittsburgh's Mattress Factory, a museum that emerged as a well-known center for installation

work during the 1980s. The result was a piece entitled *This Is/Just That* (1990–91), a work that consisted of diagrammatic drawings on the walls, floor and ceiling of the gallery. The gallery had two windows on the east and west walls of the space. These windows were frosted over, leaving some small rectangular clear openings as viewing portals to the exterior world. My intention was to make connections between the geometric drawings in the gallery and the environment outside the gallery. A small hydrostone white cone on the floor in the center of the gallery served as a focal point and corresponded to a Victorian roof that could be seen through an opening in one of the windows. Accompanying the drawings were additional graphic elements consisting of text fragments from writings by the acting theorist Stanislavski. *This Is/Just That* synthesized, in actual 3D space, graphic elements of my film works, drawings and paintings and, in retrospect, was a prototype for future computer generated installation work.

Above and facing page: From *Memory Spaces* (1994–96), a series of multi-screen stereoscopic installations by Paul Glabicki. Based on combinations of disparate European and Asian architectural elements, each projected computer-generated still image in these installations maintains basic spatial and temporal referents to create a three-dimensional illusion that is seamless, unified and dramatically surreal.

Right and facing page: From *Red Fence* (1999), an animation-installation by Paul Glabicki. The display strategy for this 3D computer animated work consists of numerous video projections distributed throughout a gallery space, all running continuously and out of synchronization. Although only one animation is used in this multi-screen installation, staggered projections create an ever-changing juxtaposition of different imagery. *Red Fence* has also been exhibited as a 60-minute single screen work at festivals and various theatrical venues.

Red Fence continues my interest in "East" and "West" as cultural contexts, as coordinates of personal memory, and as sources for opposition and dialogue. Structurally, It's like a theatrical performance with each sequence designed as an "act" in an ever-changing stage space. The early sequences are linked to some of the strategies of *Dark Room/Simple Roof*, especially its slow and deliberate pace. References to "East" are more clearly seen in these sequences. As the work progresses, western motifs become more apparent and eventually imagery from the two locations synthesize. A red fence appears in every sequence. At times it's a barrier separating the viewer from visual information, at other times it enhances the viewing process or simply becomes a minor element dominated by other objects or structures.

Hundreds of images were scanned and used as texture maps, backdrops and floating frames within scenes. The images come from a variety of sources including photographs, personal letters, travel postcards, fragments of personal paintings and drawings, old maps and illustrations. Equally diverse are the accompanying sound collages, which are composed of ambient effects, chants, classical music fragments, and so on. The imagery and soundtrack were brought together on Adobe Premiere, which provided wonderful opportunities for orchestrating rhythms and overlaying sounds. My use of computer based sound mixing and editing in *Red Fence* was a huge creative leap over the methods I used to produce film sound.

When *Red Fence* was displayed as an installation work, the physical configuration consisted of numerous video projections distributed throughout a gallery space, all running continuously and out of synchronization. In this context the piece takes on new meaning, creating complex overlays of images and different kinds of sound that change in volume as one walks through the space. Because of the work's open-ended design process, its imagery was always clear and cohesive even though the projections were out of synchronization and randomly displayed. In addition to being used in gallery situations, *Red Fence* took on another life as a 60-minute single screen work that was shown at festivals and other theatrical venues.

After *Dark Room/Simple Roof* and *Red Fence*, I became aware that my notions of animation were changing. I found myself thinking less about the single frame construction of motion and more about the broader spatial and temporal possibilities of 3D computer graphics. Unlike the 2D paper surface of my hand-made drawings, the computer monitor offered an endless volume of virtual space to inhabit and orchestrate. I assume that most artists inevitably project their imagination "into" their paper or canvas, but when working within the digital domain, space becomes incredibly tangible and real.

The mechanics of the medium are daunting – modeling, rendering, storing every bit of information – still, in spite of the inhibiting features of the medium, it's possible to produce extraordinary effects, and make the creative process intimate and personal.

Q: Your most recent animated work, *Full Moon* (2001) has been exhibited as an installation and, like *Red Fence*, has also been shown as a single channel piece. Would you describe the underlying concept of this work and the production methods used to produce both the sound and the image?

PG: Like most of my projects, *Full Moon*, developed from ideas that emerged during the previous project. My working method involved creating and linking together numerous short sequences of imagery, much as I did in *Red Fence*. In other words, *Full Moon* started with the opening title sequence and progressed from there. I never know how a piece will end, or even what it might look like at

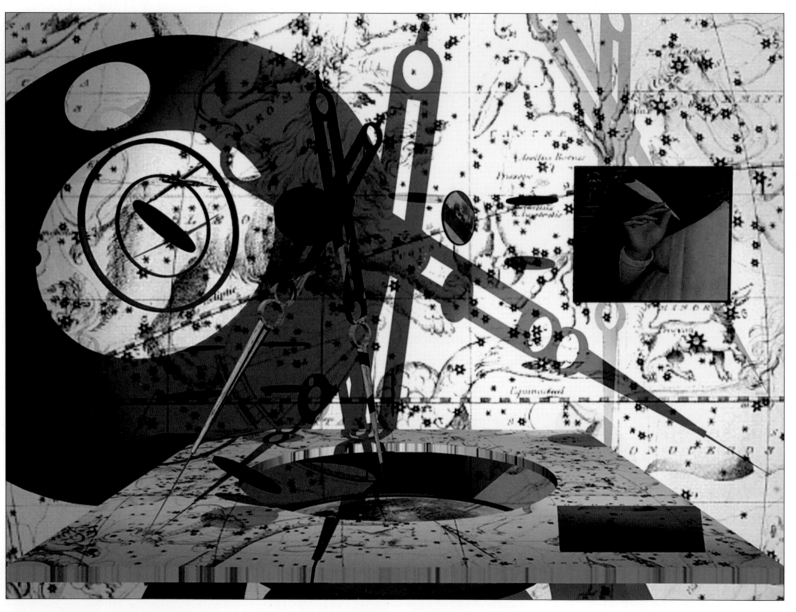

mid-point. My aim is to let the work develop while in progress. It's an open-ended approach that allows new ideas and techniques to be discovered and implemented as the piece evolves.

Preliminary work on *Full Moon*, before it even had a title, started with the gathering of images and ideas. First, I went through my own collection of stored material. I like to collect images that I'm drawn to, and then, when the need arises, use them in a project. This material can be anything from travel photographs and old postcards to recent illustrations from magazines. I also went through my personal library and gathered books that I had recently read or put aside for future reference. As I examined these materials I started to make selections, group materials, and mark chapters or pages in specific books. Technical matters dealing with how 3D computer graphics or special effects software might be used were not a consideration at this point. Content came first and would dictate the form. I eventually focused on a single image: a stereogram of a full moon photographed

Left and facing page: From *Full Moon* (2001), an animation-installation by Paul Glabicki. In this computer-generated work, Glabicki used ideas and images associated with the moon to create a multi-screen collage of cosmic visuals that is continuously organizing and deconstructing itself. In addition to being exhibited as a gallery installation, *Full Moon* has also been shown as a 41-minute single channel piece and as a virtual set for various kinds of dance and performance works.

at the Lick Observatory in Mount Hamilton, California in 1895. The stereogram, which was aged and faded, was both a record of the moon as seen by a now obsolete telescope, and a physical artifact designed to entertain and fascinate a 19th century viewer. Looking at the image was also looking back in time for over 100 years, thinking about the past and the enormous changes in human history that had occurred during a span that was hardly a blink of the eye in lunar history. The more I contemplated the stereogram, the more I thought about its meaning in terms of science, religion, myth, celestial order, gravitational pull, illumination,

and so on. It quickly became the anchor image of my piece and a constant reference for selecting and editing the materials I had gathered.

The opening animation sequence of *Full Moon* really states the thesis of the whole piece and, in a sense, encapsulates everything I thought the work was going to be about. The sequence begins with a rotating tunnel of star maps on a black background. These star maps are in the form of flat disks that are layered in space, each with a hole in the center. The computer's virtual camera actually moves forward through the center of each slowly rotating disk at great speed, covering the equivalent of miles. A full moon rises at the end of this tunnel of maps and falls backward, creating another hole into another space, a kind of celestial stage on which other moons rise and various props and objects make their first appearance. These objects are elements in a cosmic model that is continuously organizing and deconstructing itself. The sound track is layered with repetitive piano notes, industrial noise, relentless mechanical rhythms and harmonic choral phrases. The opening of the piece is designed to establish an artificial celestial construct that is fragmented and mysterious, yet provocative. The sequences that follow introduce additional objects and props and explore a wide variety of cross-cultural themes, celestial images, personal experiences and literary and religious references. The tape's final sequence, the shadow of a hand cast on the 1895 image of a full moon, is intended as a metaphor for my connection to the stereo lunar image that set the whole project in motion.

Q: How was the installation version of *Full Moon* displayed? In other words, what would a visitor to the installation see and experience?

PG: When *Full Moon* was exhibited for the first time at the Pittsburgh Center for the Arts (2001), it consisted of three separate ceiling to floor video projections, with stereo sound, arranged side by side on a large wall. A DVD transfer from a Betacam-SP sub-master permitted seamless, continuous looping of the entire 41-minute piece. All three projections were the same imagery and accompanied by the same sound, but were not synchronize with each other. The juxtaposition of animation sequences, side by side, and the overlay of the soundtracks varied every day throughout the exhibition, depending on the start and stop of each DVD player. The sound system's stereo speakers were set parallel to each projection, but behind and above the head of the viewer. As a result, the sound would seem to shift and change in volume as one moved from projection to projection. The installation had no real beginning or end and allowed viewers to stroll through the space or sit down and contemplate the images and sounds. *Full Moon*, in addition to being exhibited as a gallery installation, has been shown in a variety of other contexts including large outdoor public displays, virtual sets for dance and music performances, and as a forty-one minute single channel video piece.

Q: How have digital tools affected your production methods and was it difficult to make the transition from hand-drawn to computer-generated animation?

PG: Notwithstanding the many advantages of digital media, one has to always contend with its rapid and relentless evolution. An aggressive marketplace drives the development of hardware and software and obsolescence is a fact of life. For example, hundreds of my early Amiga files are now inaccessible. The affordability of digital media is an ongoing problem with no end in sight. Preservation of earlier formats becomes a low priority and therefore an intimate rapport with the medium has to happen quickly. Today I couldn't imagine committing four or five years to a project as I did with my film *Under the Sea*. By the time the work would be realized, its format or the equipment to display it might be obsolete. I must admit that I have adopted a philosophy of using what I have and thinking of the work as being somewhat ephemeral, existing for the moment and making way for the next moment. With the preservation of media art presently beyond the capability of any organization or archive, and the relentless development of new software and hardware a constant reality, it seems a new form of art is taking shape. One has to question whether standard art practices and traditional aesthetic values are still relevant – or are they in the process being replaced by something not yet completely identifiable?

Q: What direction has your work taken since producing *Full Moon*?

PG: Recently, I've been working on a series of drawings surrounding C.G. Jung's writings on synchronicity. The project consists of actually "transcribing" an entire book by Jung, incorporating the notion of "meaningful coincidence" throughout the space of the drawings, which include abstract and figurative images as well as diagrams. As accessible and sophisticated as software has become, there is always some frustration with converting direct hand gesture and tactile sensibility to a mouse or keyboard. There is also the incessant pressure to upgrade, digest new manuals, fund new equipment, and confront new software design that often complicates and impedes the process. Things tend to be more conscious and deliberate rather than intuitive. I have – depending on how you look at it – the advantage and burden of coming to electronic media from a background in painting, drawing, film, video and rapidly changing digital media. It can be refreshing to get back to paper, and imagery not mediated by a machine. However, I intend to return to computer animated projection pieces soon, with an initial plan to create a series of individual five-minute animation sequences/cycles on separate DVD discs. These pieces would be projected simultaneously in a multiple projection installation environment. The short time span of these pieces would allow for some anticipation or memory of each sequence and, given a large number of projections, create a continuous environment of image and sound – a kind of image/sound chorus or chant. The idea is to provide an environment or situation for observation, listening, chance juxtaposition and contemplation.

Q: What are your expectations for digital media in the years ahead?

PG: In the future I look forward to seeing much more diversity and distinctly individual work by digital artists. In particular, I look forward to new narrative forms, subtle interactive art that transcends game strategies, and new methods for the presentation and distribution of digital art. I can't help but think of the enormous range of styles that flourished during the 1960s and 70s as artists studied and worked with animation as a form of personal expression. Perhaps, as powerful digital tools continue to become more accessible and affordable to a broad range of artists, there will be a new wave of free and open experimentation. Artists can be wonderfully subversive and ingenious, and I expect that this kind of creative force will continue to emerge from time to time. I tend to be drawn to work that takes risks, opens up a new dialogue or challenges established notions of art. New forms of electronic visualization are merging art with biology, genetics and other sciences, challenging the traditional role of the artist and offering alternative approaches to the presentation and the processing of information. As an artist, I value the development of new technologies and their potential for creating fresh and expressive works. I'm not at all threatened by what I can imagine is coming, and what new art forms may emerge. I've already adapted to the idea that I will continue to do the most with what I have, that works I've created may not be subject to traditional notions of permanence and market value, and that it is becoming impossible to be completely adept at every new technical advance that comes along. I'm very curious and excited about emerging digital media, and equally willing to separate hype from artistic value. ✧

Notes

1. Non-linear projections refer to dynamic imagery that is abstract, impressionistic or interactive, as opposed to motion pictures that have a formal linear narrative.

2. Fluxus was an art movement that began in 1961 and flourished throughout the 1960s, and into the 1970s. Characterized by a strongly Dadaist attitude, Fluxus promoted artistic experimentation mixed with social and political activism. Fluxus artists used a wide range of forms and materials including mail art, sound collage, film, video, multimedia and guerilla or street theater, to challenge modernism and traditional definitions of art. Although Germany was its principal location, Fluxus was an international art movement. Artists associated with Fluxus include Joseph Beuys, Ray Johnson, Yoko Ono, Nam June Paik, Wolf Vostell and Paul Sharits, among others.

3. The term expanded cinema generally refers to the beginning of the post film era (from about 1960–80), which introduced multi-media installation works, computer and video imaging, and a host of other alternative approaches to the moving image, many of which involved the use of new technologies.

4. Arthur C. Clarke Clarke (1917–2008), science fiction writer, inventor and futurist, is the author of *2001: A Space Odyssey*. He has written numerous books and articles, both fiction and non-fiction, about the relationship between technology and society.

From a written interview, December 2002.

5 Surrogate performance and digital theatre

Using various kinds of Hyperanimation in conjunction with theatre design and performance, the artists in this chapter have contributed to a new and powerful type of public forum. Their digitally based projects have not only resulted in the fusion of compelling imagery and novel situations, but have also demonstrated a need for re-appraising the traditional stage proscenium as well as standard forms of opera, theatre and dance production. As a result, a number of very promising and provocative issues have emerged that deserve close attention. For example, what are the aesthetic implications for theatrical space when stage architecture is extended through the use of virtual panoramic scenes? In what ways can a computer-generated surrogate – a synthetic dancer, for instance – alter or expand the form and content of a performance? How can new technologies be used to create interactive visual/scenic systems and facilitate audience participation? These are but a few of the questions that have been posed by a small but innovative group of visual artists who have sought solutions through the development of new and diverse visualization techniques.

We are entering a world where there won't be one, but two realities: the actual and the virtual.
– Paul Virilio

In order to comprehend how Hyperanimation fits into the context of the theatrical arts it is important to keep in mind that certain notions about multi-media events – the melding of projected imagery, performance and interactivity – were to some extent already introduced in other contexts during the 1960s and 70s. The concept of "open systems" that could include audience participation, music and the simultaneous presentation of live and virtual elements were initially explored in experimental performance and installation art. By the 1980s techniques begun so spontaneously with these early multimedia works had infiltrated mainstream theatre, Broadway shows and stadium spectacles, especially rock music performances. This impulse to create new kinds of polysensory theatrical experiences through the use of technology went through yet another stage of development at the very end of the twentieth century when advanced computer imaging and sound generating systems emerged and offered an entirely new range of technical and expressive possibilities.

Working within a fine arts context a number of visual artists with different approaches and backgrounds became involved with digital theatre, augmenting performance projects with various forms of Hyperanimation. The pioneering works of individuals such as Paul Kaiser, the duo of Jeff Kleiser and Diana Walczak and Miroslaw Rogala, for example, have not only helped broaden the definition of media based theatre, but have indicated new directions for its future development. Other notable artists who have contributed to this field include Robert Darroll (chapter 2) who produced 3D computer animated sets for the opera, *To the Unborn Gods* (1997), and Rebecca Allen (chapter 6) known for her groundbreaking work with virtual performance. As early as 1982 Allen created a computer-generated figure that appeared with live performers in Twyla Tharp's made-for-television dance production *The Catherine Wheel*.

With the advent of new digital imaging techniques traditional methods of interpreting and recording live performance have been considerably reshaped and extended. The invention of film and video immortalized some of history's greatest dancers, preserving their movement for future generations. However, the quality of such recordings often betrays the vitality of the dancer, leaving the viewer with only a faint impression of their extraordinary ability. Motion capture – a form of 3D computer animation derived from sensors that are attached to a live performer – may very well change the dancer's predicament while at the same time providing a stylistic basis for an entirely new kind of motion graphics.

By exploiting this new technique of digitally captured movement, media artist Paul Kaiser and his associates, including artist Shelley Eshkar, have created a series of virtual dance pieces that are graphically original and deeply lyrical. Using

Facing page: From *Monsters of Grace* (1998), a digital opera by Philip Glass and Robert Wilson in collaboration with animators Jeff Kleiser and Diana Walczak. [© 1998 International Production Associates; image courtesy Kleiser-Walczak.]

Right: From *Ghostcatching* (1999), a virtual dance installation produced by Paul Kaiser and Shelley Eshkar in association with dancer and choreographer Bill T. Jones.
[© Bill T. Jones, Paul Kaiser, Shelley Eshkar.]

an approach that has neither the solid look of motion captured cartoon imagery, nor traditional hand-drawn character animation, Kaiser's hyperanimated works assume the essence of human movement and place it in another context, a visual reality expressed through the eloquence and elegance of line. Although the linear figure drawings that compose his works are programmed by the computer, they do not have an android-like presence, but rather a free and gestural type of movement that has weight, purpose and a surprisingly emotional quality. With digital pieces such as *Hand-drawn Spaces* (1998), *Ghostcatching* (1999) and *Biped* (1999), Kaiser has proven that it is possible to develop alternatives to the mainstream 3D computer animation approach and to create fluid and expressive abstractions of the human figure in motion. In *Ghostcatching*, Kaiser's much acclaimed video installation, a seamless and mesmerizing projected loop of figurative contours in motion are shown life-size on a large screen. Produced in collaboration with a small team of collaborators and celebrated choreographer-performer Bill T. Jones, the work displays the essential qualities of human movement through line drawings that are abstract and minimal, yet clearly legible as dance language. The actual production process began by tracking Jones' dance movements with the aid of a computer and customized software. The captured data files reflected the position and rotation of Jones as he moved without retaining the performer's actual physical mass. Movement, in a sense, was extracted from Jones' anatomy, digitized, and used as a building block for the animation. Phrases of the captured performance were then edited and computer generated gesture drawings were created to serve as a virtual surrogate for Jones' body. The sound track of *Ghostcatching* consists of grunts, cries, speaking, singing and electronically manipulated effects that represent the sound of limbs slicing through the air. The animation that is ultimately projected onto the screen has the velocity and character of a rapidly rendered charcoal drawing. The imagery, however, was created entirely in the computer. No paper or conventional art materials were involved. Through the pure power of line, the dance imagery of *Ghostcatching* never appears to be inscribed on a flat surface like an ordinary drawing, but instead has a strange kind of volumetric quality, in effect, a transparent three-dimensionality that is characterized by rotating forms and changing perspectives. The virtual dancers – generations of figures that stem from Jones' performance work – move in an environment that has no ground, no atmosphere and no physical tension. Still, there exists on the screen a palpable and fascinating sense of space in which these calligraphic figures leap, bend, reach and even appear to interact with each other. *Ghostcatching* is about the alignment of dance and visual art, it is a dynamic virtual stage where human movement is transformed into an absorbing hyper-animated artwork that can be viewed and examined in all its complexity.

In *Biped*, a piece that immediately followed *Ghostcatching*, Kaiser again created dance imagery using motion capture technology, but this time the animation was projected in conjunction with live performers in a theatrical setting. The basic layout of the work, which was designed and produced in collaboration with renowned choreographer Merce Cunningham, consisted of multiple screens for the projection of animation, including a large scrim that covered the front of the proscenium. During the performance live dancers shared the stage with virtual dancers, activating and reorganizing the space as they moved in and among the animated images. An innovative work, both technically and artistically, *Biped* points the way to a new direction in the art making process, a type of collaboration in which dancers and digital artists can explore hybrid forms of expression in a theatrical context.

Jeff Kleiser and Diana Walczak, pioneers in the development of 3D digital imaging techniques became a team in 1985, specializing in high-end computer animation for film, television and stereoscopic theme park attractions. They temporarily departed from their usual animation work in 1997 to collaborate with Philip Glass and Robert Wilson on the production of a digital opera entitled

Monsters of Grace. Based on a text by a thirteenth century Persian mystic, Jeladdin Rumi, *Monsters of Grace* is a combination of music, live stage action and stereoscopic computer animated projections. It is not an opera in the traditional sense, nor are the 3D animated projections like the type of action-packed stereoscopic imagery produced purely for entertainment purposes. Rather, *Monsters of Grace* is a highly abstract yet emotionally engaging work, a combination of slow-moving imagery and trance-like music that produces a non-narrative experience that is dream-like and conducive to meditation. Weaving back and forth between illusion and reality, live performance and projected images, the opera invites the audience to explore its provocative and multi-sensory content, to make connections between the visual and musical components, and to construct their own personal interpretation. The thirteen scenes that comprise the opera were not designed to tell a story or to illustrate the lyrics and music, but instead, they were intended to be viewed the way one would look at a series of separate paintings. The temporal structure of the scenes, therefore, has an impressionistic and non-linear quality, intentionally avoiding the type of sound-image synchronization found in traditional animation. All of the opera's imagery

Above: From *Nature is Leaving Us* (1989), a video theatre performance written, composed and directed by Miroslaw Rogala.
[Photo documentation courtesy of Rogala Studio/Outerpretation, Chicago, Illinois.]

Paul Kaiser

Media artist Paul Kaiser, with experimental animator Shelly Eshkar and other associates, has developed a unique approach to creating expressive graphic representations of the human body moving in time and space. Collaborating with choreographers Merce Cunningham and Bill T. Jones, on separate projects, Kaiser and his team used customized motion capture techniques to produce lyrical and highly stylized forms of animated dance imagery.

In *Hand-drawn Spaces*, a large three-screen installation created in conjunction with Cunningham in 1998, live dancers were translated via motion capture into graceful linear drawings. These drawings were then combined and overlaid

in the computer, exploiting the expressive possibilities of a virtual world that has no ties to the physical environment. In another collaborative project with Cunningham entitled *Biped* (1999), motion capture was again used, but this time the dance animation that resulted was shown in a theatrical context, a stage performance that integrated a projection of digitally generated dancers with live choreography.

Ghostcatching (1999), acclaimed as a landmark in the computerized rendering of human form, was produced in collaboration with dancer Bill T. Jones. In this work Jones's physical form was replaced by generations of ethereal surrogates, calligraphic figure drawings that moved fluidly in three-dimensional space. A looping eight-and-a-half minute single-screen display composed of digitally portrayed synthetic dancers, *Ghostcatching* not only expands the artistry of Kaiser's and Eshkar's previous works with motion capture, but opens up future possibilities for both the technique of animation and choreographic expression.

Born in 1956, Paul Kaiser received a BA from Wesleyan University in Connecticut in 1978, followed by a M.Ed. degree in special education from American University in Washington, DC in 1983. His early work was in experimental filmmaking and performance audiotapes. Kaiser later spent ten years teaching students with severe learning disabilities with whom he collaborated on making multi-media works that earned him a Computer World/Smithsonian Award in 1991. In 1994 he founded Riverbed in New York, a production studio specializing in digital media, and was joined by his associate Shelly Eshkar in 1995. The first interactive artist to receive a Guggenheim Fellowship, Kaiser has been a visiting lecturer and faculty member at a number of institutions including San Francisco State University, California; Wesleyan University, Connecticut and Harvard's Graduate School of Design in Cambridge, Massachusetts.

Interview with PAUL KAISER

Q: In the early stages of your career you were an experimental filmmaker and teacher. At what point did you become seriously interested in 3D computer animation and the technique of motion capture?

Paul Kaiser: I became interested in 3D animation around 1990, several years before I actually started working in it. The first idea I had about its application was the notion of "hand-drawn space", that is, the paradoxical idea that one might be able to model and render a 3D space with the openness and lyricism of drawing rather than the rigidity and detail of CAD and photorealistic rendering. To a large extent my interest in 3D was driven by the sterility that I saw in the field – a field that seemed to have ignored the history of 20th century visual art.

My understanding of 3D deepened tremendously when I met computer animators Michael Girard and Susan Amkraut, who soon became very good friends of mine. This was in about 1992 and before they'd started work on their figure animation software *Biped*, which later turned into *Character Studio*. In addition to educating me about the field of 3D computer animation they also encouraged me to pursue my notion of hand-drawn space.

However, it wasn't until 1995–96 that I managed to create the first hand-drawn test, working with a young man here in NYC named Nam Szeto. The animation was a crude walkthrough of a Robert Wilson notebook drawing, which despite its flaws demonstrated that the concept could definitely be achieved. Shortly afterwards I started working with Shelley Eshkar, who solved many of the shortcomings in the original test through sophisticated use of splines rather than planes & solids.

Around the same time, Michael and Susan's figure animation program went into alpha, which gave me the idea of marrying my hand-drawn idea with dance. I then approached Merce Cunningham about the possibility of doing a project together and had the great good fortune of obtaining his interest.

The technique of motion capture only entered the picture after we started the project and we realized the impracticality of trying to key frame a dance. For one thing we found that we couldn't capture some of the subtler nuances – imperfections even – of human performance; key framed motions were not only incredibly laborious, they became *too* perfect. Michael went to work on expanding *Character Studio* to read motion-capture data, and we immediately shifted the project to working that way.

Q: What is Riverbed and how did it get started?

PK: Nowadays Riverbed is a studio consisting of two and a half people: myself, Shelley Eshkar, and my wife Kathy Kaiser, our business manager. Its purpose is to fund and support our artworks. Originally Riverbed was set up in 1994 with three partners: myself and two others, one a young entrepreneur, the other a highly successful author and publisher. Eventually only I remained when it became clear that my interest was in steering the studio in an artistic direction, rather than doing commercial projects.

Q: Your work with animation has been concerned with computer mediated drawing as a form

of performance, with a recent concentration on the creative possibilities of virtual dance. What, specifically, attracted you to the art of dance as a subject for your work?

PK: Part of it was accidental. I met William Forsythe, the director of the Frankfurt Ballet, who opened up the incredibly rich world of choreography to me. I had long been interested in movement *per se*; indeed the last Super-8 film I'd made in 1977 was a study of pedestrian movement at a New York City intersection. But now I was able to see dance through the eyes of extraordinary choreographers. As a dance interloper over the years I've had tremendous luck in getting to know not only Forsythe, but also Cunningham and Bill T. Jones, three of the greatest

intention were absent from this choreographic process, for Merce used chance operation to see what phrase went next. Here as elsewhere, his art was all about movement, his interest absorbed by how the dancing worked in space and time. He had no qualms about motion-capture or computer composition or hand-drawn rendering, all seen as different means to the same end he'd been pursuing for the past fifty years. Not so Bill T. Jones.

"I do not want to be a disembodied, denatured, de-gendered series of lines moving in a void", he said. Whereas *Hand-drawn Spaces* reveled in the freedom of abstracted motion, *Ghostcatching* would question it.

... Before we could start, Bill had to have twenty-four markers taped to his body. He looked balefully at these markers, and then at the lights, the cameras, the tripods, the screens – at all the technology of reproduction surrounding him – and said he felt he was breaking a taboo. "Dancers have a strange piety", he said, "a romantic notion that only the ephemeral moment of performance counts". To the purist, recording was a blasphemy – like some people not wanting their picture taken for fear of losing their soul. He said we were "ghostcatching", and the name stuck. Bill asked how so few markers could possibly capture all his motion. His dancing was not so angular as Merce's, he explained, not a matter solely of the skeleton and of the angles it took, but also of the undulation and quivering of liquid muscle.

He was right. I had never seen Bill dance before, but now as he started, careful at first with all the markers stuck to him, I saw he was right. He glanced down at the Xeroxed photos we'd placed on the floor, and then he improvised sequences connecting one pose to the next. Six times he ran through the series, each improvisation freer and more fluid than the last. As his exuberance took over, the sweat poured out of him and some of the markers popped off of him. Bill's dance did ripple in waves through his body as his weight kept shifting, and it was true that some of his motion would be near impossible to capture.

Yet afterwards even he could see that the moving dots on the computer screen had caught some sort of essence. "*Who* am I looking at?" was his first question. Then he said if anyone was to reconstitute his movements in the year 2040, this was how they would do it. Later, he told us it was like the first time you saw the back of your head in a mirror, and said, "Ah, so *that's* what I look like!"

... Only long after we started working together did Bill and I discover our common artistic roots in avant-garde film. Here my major debt was to Robert Breer, an animator most famous for making films in which few "shots" were longer than a frame. He disdained traditional keyframe animation, which created a continuous simulation of life through thousands of gradually modified drawings.

screens. People had to crane their necks and stretch their minds to track the momentarily invisible crossings back and forth between the screens, as sounds of footsteps and breathing – and, at the end, of Ron Kuivila's deafening electronic music – seemed to move right through them.

A curious thing about *Hand-drawn Spaces*: the movements we captured were truly detached from the dancers who had so brilliantly performed them, Jeannie Steele and Jared Phillips. The differences between the two in size and sex and style were annulled as Merce combined their captured phrases freely, making long passages in which one dancer's movements alternated frequently with the other's, both mapped to the same hand-drawn figure. Psychology and

In that work-flow, the key poses are set first, and the smooth "in-betweens" are added later.

Ghostcatching relied on continuous keyframed animation for its fidelity to dance. But there was another aspect of Breer that corresponded closely – his revival of rotoscoping.

In this early method of extracting motion from a figure, the animator traces live action footage frame by frame, so that only certain lines of the moving figure remain. In Breer's hands, the results were exquisite. For *Gulls and Buoys* (1972), he rotoscoped a brief shot of his daughter walking on the seashore. His rough crayon tracings jerked with the imprecision of his hand, but they also moved with the underlying grace of the girl, so that the motions of the artist drawing and of his subject walking seemed to fuse. Since the grain of the crayon wax matched the grain of the film stock, and the rotoscoped waves crumpled in time with the flickering projector, there was a wonderful unity. The image stayed with me ever since.

Breer's other influence was more accidental. When I came to know Bob years later, he was a professor at Cooper Union, where he introduced me to his best students. One of them was Shelley, whose eventual hand-drawn animation methods owed nothing technically to rotoscoping, yet had much of the same spirit.

... In *Hand-drawn Spaces*, moving figures were all we needed. We cast their reflections on the floor, which became the only visible trace of a world beyond them. The reflections made the footfalls and jumps more palpable; they accentuated the depth of that world, while reasserting the two-dimensionality of the screen. Were they reflections or shadows? In our drawn world they could be either.

In *Ghostcatching* the visible world also emanates from the dancers, but goes further. In the beginning we see an ancestral figure enclosed in a tight-fitting box, cycling through a loop of poses. He is made up of the same simple lines and planes as the box, which measures his body's cubic volume. Does the box hold the dancer in place or does it mark the place the dancer holds to, locked in his keyframed loop? Is it his kinesphere or his coffin? Elsewhere we see dancers drawing lines in space with their graceful trajectories. When these marks harden and persist, new dancers unravel from the skein, but they too leave their traces, choking the space and capturing the dancers within it.

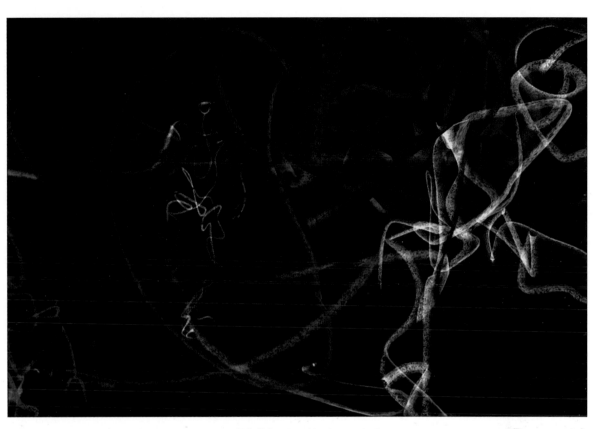

Moving on, we see a dancer more aware of his reflection. He dances before a mirror, that more ordinary and fleeting means of capture seen in every dance studio. It invites a more natural and intimate partnering.

And at the finale we see multiplied dancers moving as a single complex body. Lines tethering them together seem to propagate phase-shifting motions among them until it all fades out into infinite possibility.

We've never left the notions of mental space and drawing as performance. ... But *Ghostcatching* is a different sort of mental space. It arises from several minds all at once. Its meaning lies between us – not only between those of us who made it, but also those who now see it. It's collaboration, and it could never have been anything else.

Above and facing page: From *Ghostcatching* (1999) by Paul Kaiser and Shelley Eshkar in association with Bill T. Jones.
[© Bill T. Jones, Paul Kaiser, Shelley Eshkar.]

Jeff Kleiser and Diana Walczak

In 1997 animators Jeff Kleiser and Diana Walczak collaborated with Philip Glass and Robert Wilson, co-directing an entirely computer-generated 70mm stereo-scopic film for the digital opera, *Monsters of Grace*. The result was a high-tech stage performance that not only broke barriers in the technical innovation and production of stereoscopic animation, but also opened up a new and promising direction in the field of music theatre – the use of dynamic three-dimensional imagery rather than painted sets and physical props. Conceived by Wilson and designed by Kleiser-Walczak Construction Co., each animated scene of the opera offers a sumptuous play of 3D spatial imagery, color and movement that contributes to seventy-five minutes of brilliant and evocative fantasy. *Monsters of Grace*, which has toured worldwide, held its world premiere in April 1998 at Royce Hall in Los Angeles, California.

Jeff Kleiser has contributed to many milestones in the motion industry and his pioneering work in the field of digital imaging has spanned the history of the medium. He was a founding partner and president of Digital Effects, New York City's first computer animation company, supervising animation for Disney's *Blue Lagoon* (1980), *Tron* (1982) and numerous other commercial projects. Later, as director of the motion picture special effects division of Omnibus Computer Graphics, Kleiser supervised the first "morphing" in feature films for Disney's *Flight of the Navigator* (1986). He has also been involved in the production of animation for theme park rides, most notably the Kleiser-Walczak stereoscopic production of *The Amazing Adventures of Spider-Man*, which was installed in 1999 at Universal Studios in Florida. For this project a new stereo ("squinching") technol-ogy was developed that enabled riders to experience a seamless series of 3D films while traveling throughout the installation. In addition to his digital production work in the motion picture industry, Kleiser also teaches computer animation at Williams College in Massachusetts. He has presented papers about his projects and technical achievements at numerous events including Siggraph, Institut de l'Audiovisuel (INA), Imagina, the National Association of Broadcasters (NAB) and the Virtual Humans Conference.

Animator and special effects artist Diana Walczak studied engineering and computer science at Boston University and finished with a degree in sculpture in 1985. After working as a medical illustrator, she was hired by Omnibus Computer Graphics to sculpt a super hero figure for a Marvel Comics' 3D animation test, an experience that marked the beginning of her career in digital imaging. In 1987, shortly after joining Jeff Kleiser to form Kleiser-Walczak Construction Co., the duo created two award-winning shorts that are regarded as milestones in the history of computer graphics. Both films, *Nestor Sextone for President* (1988) and *Don't Touch Me* (1989) involved the use of SynthespianSM performers, an approach to 3D character animation recognized for its contribution to the evolution of computer-generated humans. Kleiser-Walczak coined the brand name Syn-thespianSM (synthetic actor) in 1989 to describe their studio's method of creating 3D animated characters that move in a believable life-like manner. During her career Walczak has directed and co-directed numerous commercial projects, receiving a Clio Award for the thirty-second spot entitled *Trophomotion* in 1999. Before assuming the role of director she served as animation supervisor for the PBS series *The Astronomers* (1991), as well as for feature motion pictures such as *Stargate* (1994) and *Judge Dredd* (1995). In 2002 Walczak was appointed to a Federal Commission, formed by the Departments of Education and Commerce to study how technology might be harnessed in the future to revitalize methods of education.

Interview with JEFF KLEISER

Q: How did you become involved with computer animation and what circumstances brought you and Diana together to form Kleiser-Walczak Construction Company?

Jeff Kleiser: While I was at Colgate University during the early 1970s majoring in math, I was required to take some sort of computer course as part of the core curriculum. I enrolled in a computer music course and immediately became intrigued with the idea of using the computer for creative purposes. I soon became less interested in math and more interested in being a computer science major. Colgate at that time offered a special studies program during the month of January that gave students an opportunity to do something experimental and get course credit for it. I decided to use that month to go to Syracuse, which is about an hour away from Colgate, and work for IBM. I wanted to study the company's operation, its approach to sales, maintenance and engineering, and find out if I was interested in computer science as a possible career. As it turned out, I discovered that I wasn't at all interested in what IBM had to offer. However, while I was there I happened to live in an apartment below a professor who taught at Syracuse University's School of Communication and who was making short 16mm computer-generated films. He was using a form of wire frame animation to create various kinds of kinetic mandalas and geometric abstract patterns. I got to know him and became very interested in what he was doing. In fact, he became a mentor of mine and actually helped me to create a computer graphics major at Colgate by providing the help and software I needed to develop my own curriculum, do research and make films. As a result, I was able to have a major that was located somewhere between computer science and fine arts and get experience in a new field that otherwise would not have been possible.

When I left college in 1976 I went to New York and studied Holography for a while. However, I soon found that holography as a medium really wasn't going to give me the visual capability that I was hoping for, meaning seventy foot images that could be viewed from multiple directions and that created an illusion of real depth. The medium had far too many limitations and that type of scale just wasn't possible. At about that time, Judson Rosebush, my mentor from Syracuse and some of his associates decided to start a company to pursue computer animation. They all moved down to New York and together we set up a company called Digital Effects. I worked in a special effects laboratory during the day, which involved conventional motion picture film techniques – matte work, models, miniatures – and then at night I would work with Judson Rosebush and his team at the company we formed. There were seven of us doing computer animation. As it turned out my day job at the special effects laboratory provided technical support for my night job, allowing me access to the optical equipment we needed to get images from the computer onto film. We were the first company to do computer animation in New York. We wrote our own software, did a lot of commercials, and were one of four companies that produced computer animation for the Disney feature film, *Tron*. The company started in 1978 and *Tron* was made around 1980. By 1985 we had exhausted our ability to work together

effectively. The company consisted of seven people with equal stock in the company and it was not a viable arrangement. Everybody had a different idea of what we should be doing. We dissolved the company and I went to work for Omnibus Computer Graphics in 1985.

I met Diana Walczak at Siggraph 85 in San Francisco. She was an artist and sculptor and was interested in finding ways to apply her abilities to the computer graphics field. At that time I was working on a project at Omnibus for Marvel Comics and trying to figure out a more effective way to create a 3D computer generated figure. Together, Diana and I developed a technique for digitizing a three-dimensional object using Diana's sculpture as the basis for the human form. The Marvel Comics project fell through but Diana kept working with us at Omnibus to develop the techniques we needed to make 3D computer-generated characters.

Above: From *Monsters of Grace* (1998), a digital opera by Philip Glass and Robert Wilson in collaboration with animators Jeff Kleiser and Diana Walczak. Throughout this 74-minute theatrical performance a 35mm stereoscopic animated film is projected on stage creating a large scale virtual environment, a dynamic and evocative world composed of surreal 3D computer-generated imagery.
[© 1998 International Production Associates, image courtesy Kleiser-Walczak.]

Right: From right to left, Robert Wilson, Diana Walczak and Jeff Kleiser in a planning session for *Monsters of Grace*. [© 1998 International Production Associates, image courtesy Kleiser-Walczak.]

Unfortunately, Omnibus went out of business in 1986 and at that point Diana and I decided we would start our own company, which would focus on 3D computer-generated character animation. We built the company up carefully and eventually it expanded to three sites: Los Angeles, New York and our facility at MASS MoCA (Massachusetts Museum of Contemporary Art)[1] in the Berkshires.

While we were at our original location in Los Angeles we worked on several big projects: one was a television series for a PBS called *The Astronomers*. We created special effects for that series, mainly a lot of cosmic phenomena, and that caught the eye of Douglas Trumbull. Trumbull, who was a special effects supervisor for Stanley Kubrick's *2001* and Ridley Scott's *Blade Runner* had moved to the Berkshires in Western Massachusetts to pursue visual effects on his own terms rather than on Hollywood's terms. He was involved in producing these elaborate entertainment rides within motion picture environments and, at that time, had a contract with Luxor Hotel in Las Vegas to do three of them. He wanted to use a lot of computer animation in these new rides but he didn't have any expertise in that area. When he went to Hollywood to look into computer animation, he heard about our company, saw our work on *The Astronomers* project, and arranged to meet us. After hearing about his project, which involved mixing live-action with computer animation, Diane and I felt that the only practical approach was to do it all in the Berkshires. We didn't think it was feasible to do computer animation in Los Angeles, shoot film of models at his facility in the Berkshires, and expect it to all match up. We told him we would be willing to pack up our stuff, hire the best people in the business and set up everything at his place to do these projects for Luxor. He agreed. We came to the Berkshires and did the projects. After they were completed Doug sold his company and facility

to Synergy Productions. Synergy was under contract to do the special effects – models and animation – for the feature film, *Judge Dredd*. We stayed on and did all of the computer animation for that project. Then we went back to L.A., opened a facility and shortly afterward did the computer-generated effects for the film, *Star Gate*. After working in L.A. for a while we decided to move back to the Berkshires and make MASS MoCA our main facility for computer modeling and animation.

Q: Your early interest in holography seems to presage your later 3D stereoscopic film projects, particularly *Monsters of Grace*. Would you discuss your interest in spatial imaging and how you became involved with holography?

JK: I began working with holography in college. There was a physics laboratory at Colgate with some lasers sitting around and I experimented a little bit, but didn't really get serious about it until I got to New York and met some people in Soho who were doing advanced technical work with plate holograms. It's an interesting medium and the idea of making images that actually appear to exist in space was intriguing to me from the very beginning. I had hoped, at the time, to make holograms from 3D computer generated graphics rather than using the standard technique of recording real subject matter, but of course that didn't happen. I talk periodically with Steve Benton at the Massachusetts Institute of Technology (MIT) and he says they're doing it now. Although a lot of progress has been made in the field I have yet to see a computer-calculated hologram that's really impressive. Anyway, my idea back then was to link 3D computer animation to a holographic output and create these amazing large-scale moving images that appear to exist in real space. They would have 180-degree perspective changes and could be seen without special glasses or any other kind of stereo viewing device. It would be like looking through a real window. As yet, of course, that's not technically possible, but as research continues maybe something of this type will be developed in the future.

Q: Would you discuss your collaboration with Philip Glass and Robert Wilson and how Kleiser-Walczak became involved in their digital opera, *Monsters of Grace*?

JK: The producer of *Monsters of Grace*, Jed Wheeler, was friends with someone working at the MASS MOCA complex and he came up to North Adams from New York to visit and look around. At the time, most of MASS MoCA was still under construction, but we had moved into the second floor of one of the buildings and were ensconced there when Jed came to town. When he arrived we were doing the initial design work and stereoscopic testing for the *Spiderman* theme park ride that would later be installed at Universal Studios. We knew all about producing computer generated stereo imagery from the work we did on the Luxor Hotel rides with Doug Trumbull. Anyway, when Jed visited our studio we showed him some stereo pairs of the *Spiderman* project. By looking through a hand-held viewer he could see the *Spiderman* tests and the three-dimensional stereo effect. He told us about a project that he was trying to develop, but didn't know how in the world he could do it. He went on to say that Bob Wilson and Phil Glass were way overboard in the design of a new opera they were doing called, *Monsters of Grace*. I was familiar with Phil's music and had heard about their earlier opera, *Einstein on the Beach*, but had never seen it. Jed said they were designing things that he had no idea how to stage or finance. One of the more difficult effects that he mentioned involved this enormous physically constructed foot that would be slowly lowered down onto the stage. This idea had been laid out in Bob's sketches for the opera's stage design. Jed told us he couldn't afford to build and transport this foot and furthermore didn't know how many theaters in the world could actually accommodate it. He thought for a moment and said, "Maybe with this 3D projection gizmo you guys could do a foot". I told him all we would need is

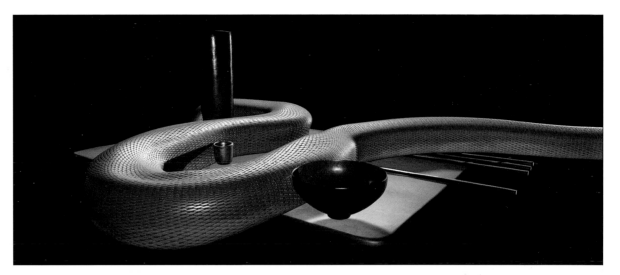

two projectors and a screen on stage. The audience would have to wear polarized glasses, but they would see a volumetric three-dimensional foot come down and it could be as big as Bob wanted it to be. Then Diana said, "Why don't we just do the whole opera using stereo imagery instead of a set. We could have a screen behind Phil's ensemble and the vocalists and project the whole thing." And I thought to myself – the opera is seventy-four minutes long. It just wouldn't be feasible. Jed, however, felt it was a really interesting idea and said he would talk to Phil and Bob about it.

Actually, both Diana and I thought there was little chance that our proposal would be accepted. Who would be crazy enough to consider something like that? As it turned out Bob and Phil, to our surprise, were interested and so Diana and I went down to New York and arranged to show them some stereoscopic footage at the Warner Bros. Building. It was a stereo version of a Bugs Bunny cartoon and we all put on polarized glasses and viewed it. I felt like such an idiot watching this cartoon with Robert Wilson, but it was the only thing we could get our hands on quickly to demonstrate our idea. After the screening I immediately explained, "that's a cartoon, that's not the type of thing we're going to do for your opera". Then we showed Bob some stereo *Spiderman* slides, which were only slightly more appropriate, but he understood the process and was intrigued with the idea of working with a new medium. So Bob, Phil and Jed got together and told us how much money they could dedicate to the stereo animation project and asked if we could do it. Our initial reaction was that they hadn't budgeted nearly enough money. However, we noticed that the designs for the thirteen scenes were exceedingly simple and that we wouldn't have to produce seventy-four minutes of what we normally do, which is very complicated, fast-moving animated action.

Above: Still life with Japanese pottery and snake. A scene from *Monsters of Grace*. [© 1998 International Production Associates, image courtesy Kleiser-Walczak.]

Left: Audience wears special stereo glasses while attending a performance of *Monsters of Grace* at the UCLA Center for the Performing Arts, 15 April 1998. [© 1998 International Production Associates, image courtesy Kleiser-Walczak.]

technology progressed I began to explore other possibilities and eventually computer imaging became an integral part of my multimedia projects.

A fellowship in 1983 and an equipment grant in 1984 provided funding that allowed me to improve my studio facilities and buy a computer that ran a Z-Grass animation program. I personally made some modifications to the system, upgrading the display memory from 16 to 64 screens, which was a big deal at the time. I also began working with Image Processors, electronic visualization devices designed by Dan Sandin (see chapter 6) that were capable of colorizing and graphically manipulating video and animation.

To program all of this new equipment, I worked in close collaboration with John Friedman and Joe Reitzer, and we were joined later by Darrell Moore. As my multimedia work developed and became more complex, other artists and performers including John Boesche, Dieter Froese, Lucien Vector and Urszula Dudziak became involved in the collaborative process, contributing to projects such as *Remote Faces: Outerpretation* (1986), *Nature Is Leaving Us* (1989) and *Lovers Leap* (1995), as well as my more recent large scale interactive public works.

Q: *Nature Is Leaving Us* **is one of your best-known video theatre works. Would you describe its layout, the configuration of the stage, and how the live performance component of this work is integrated with the large-scale display of videowall imagery and slide projections?**

idea of creating a sense of being overwhelmed is an important part of my aesthetic message. I work at the edge of the content curve. What is the minimum amount of time needed to perceive an image, an idea or a sequence? How do viewers process this high-energy experience and to what extent does each member of the audience perceive it differently?

MR: The physical requirements necessary for performing this piece are an open stage on which there are placed contiguously three sixteen-monitor videowalls,

Q: **During those early years in Chicago you also began working with computer technology. At what point did you become interested in programming and digital media?**

MR: In the late 1970s, the metropolitan area of Chicago had emerged as a major center for art and technology. It was an exciting place to be at that time and I became very interested in the possibility of using these new forms of digital media that were becoming available. So at the same time I was producing video and performance works in the early 1980s, I was also beginning to learn about computers and computer programming. At first I used the computer primarily as a drawing tool, outputting my images to paper and film with a plotter. These early computer-generated drawings mainly consisted of preliminary studies and sketches for large-scale installation projects. However, as my work with digital

four monitors high by four monitors wide. This scale is important because it established the height of the video as roughly equal to the height of a man. Although each separate videowall is capable of playing separate images to separate monitors or combinations of monitors, *Nature Is Leaving Us* used each video wall to display a single full grid image. Three separate videotapes, one for each video wall, are run synchronously with each other. Because each video wall abuts the other, a single four by twelve rectangle of monitors can be created on which I could display one large single image by joining the three video channels. At other times the center channel might present one set of images while the two side channels could contain separate synchronized images. The videowalls run continuously throughout the performance and the composite panorama of the three channels in conjunction with each other provide for a variety of design and sequencing possibilities.

The videowalls were placed about twenty feet from the front edge of the stage to create a space that accommodates up to six performers who enter at various times from the left or the right. Slides are projected onto a screen above the videowalls, extending the viewing area and adding an additional layer of imagery. Other features include audio speakers that are placed throughout the theatre, surrounding the audience and creating a 360 degree movement of sound, plus various kinds of props, objects and instruments that are brought on and off the stage at different times during the performance as required. Each section of the piece deals with a specific aspect of man's relationship to nature or a specific phase of human development. My aim was to create experiential models that were concerned with certain dynamic aspects of human existence and the environment. Each section of the performance is designed to present a different paradigm for thinking or dreaming about the world.

Q: Would you discuss the underlying concept of *Nature Is Leaving Us* and the various artistic, technical and social issues that are addressed and explored in this work?

MR: *Nature Is Leaving Us* is designed to confront the audience, in a sense interrogating them about our contemporary approach to nature and its conflicting relationship with urban life. Contemporary human existence is seen as a polyphony that involves the opposing relationship of urbanity and the features of nature; the primitive, the wild, the accidental. The work is a series of combined actions and situations and is intended as a metaphor for the simultaneity of experience that is modern life. Composed of concurrent provocations and contrasting rhythms, the overall presentation is a complex structure of images, music, vocalizations, poetry, performance and dance. The panoramic imagery

displayed on the videowalls is extended in real space by performance and dance; each of the elements is an independent but ecologically related part of the dialogue.

Although I usually refer to *Nature Is Leaving Us* as a work of video theatre, I also think of it as a video opera. In opera, a vocal libretto is set to music. My libretto is comprised of live and video elements: texts, monologues, dialogues, dance, performance and pictorial displays. The music and sound effects are designed to accompany and counterpoint the images and performances, and are analogous to the functions of the score in a traditional opera. The entire piece was conceived as a whole and I composed the sound component and media libretto simultaneously, building up each element individually. The fourteen distinct sections that are used to organize the vast ground covered by the opera were conceived as a metaphor, referring to the biblical idea that it took seven days and seven nights to create the world.

Q: The composition of elements in scene XII is particularly interesting and very unusual. Would you discuss the type of relationship and interactivity that takes place between the videowall and the stage performance in this section of the piece?

MR: Scene XII is called *The Electronic City* and it's a totally machine-based presentation. Even the onstage activities in this section were by machines rather than human performers. During this scene all three video channels were a dense texture of pure electronic noise that had been recorded onto magnetic tape and then tinted a leafy green. Although the imagery was abstract it had a digital resemblance to the space and structure of the urban world. The surround sound

Above and facing page: From *Nature is Leaving Us* (1989), a video theatre performance written, composed and directed by Miroslaw Rogala. An open-ended multimedia work, this stage production addresses a wide range of issues including the emerging electronic landscape, prevailing attitudes about nature and the rapid transformation of contemporary life.
[Photo documentation courtesy of Rogala Studio/Outerpretation, Chicago, Illinois.]

6 Virtual environments

Each age finds its own technique.
– *Jackson Pollack*

A display connected to a digital computer gives us a chance to gain familiarity with concepts not realizable in the physical world. It is a looking glass into a mathematical wonderland.
– *Dr. Ivan Sutherland*

There are now advanced forms of visualization technology that can convince a viewer that he or she is immersed in an alternative environment, experiencing an event that does not physically exist in the so-called real world. This technology, which is generally referred to as virtual reality (VR), allows the viewer to enter a digitally constructed environment, look around, move throughout the space and interact with the surroundings. A viewer, for instance, can visit places that simulate the natural world, traverse abstract geometric landscapes or interact with exotic creatures in surrealistic locations. These experiences are completely illusory, in effect, the theatre of the mind.

As futuristic as VR may seem, it is not entirely new – nor is it merely some kind of entertaining novelty. Rather, it is a contemporary manifestation of an enduring innate urge to create art works that are immersive and polysensory. An interest in environmental aesthetic experiences can be traced through nearly all epochs of art history. Recent examples of this age-old tendency range from the Wagnerian concept of the *Gesamtkunstwerk* and Sergei Eisenstein's theories of multisensory 3D movies, to the intermedia art performances and expanded cinema of the 1960s and 70s. The impulse to develop more complex illusionistic effects continued through the latter part of the twentieth century with a variety of presentation methods including wide-screen cinema, holography and stereoscopic IMAX-movies. All of the new technological display systems had essentially the same aim: to immerse the onlooker deeper and deeper into the image. As forms of artistic visualization they represented an ongoing search for a richer illusion, using the most advanced methods available in order to more fully address the human sensorium.

With the invention of the head-mounted display (HMD) by computer scientist Ivan Sutherland in the mid-1960s, a radically new perceptual dimension was introduced to the ongoing development of visualization technology. For the first time in history a viewer could become totally immersed in a dynamic virtual image. By constructing a device that contained small viewing screens (one placed in front of each eye for the stereoscopic effect), Sutherland made it possible for a user to enter the space of the computer and to visually examine images and objects on a quantitatively different level. The virtual world created by the computer and viewed via a HMD had the sensation of real depth; furthermore it was not bound by a rectangle like a painting, photograph or film, but rather appeared in any direction the viewer chose to look. Sutherland's viewing system, albeit a laboratory model, was fully immersive virtual reality: only the stereoscopic computer image was visible to the user.

As other scientists and research centers (most notable NASA) began investigating Sutherland's concept, his viewing equipment went through a series of permutations and improvements. In 1984 Jaron Lanier (who coined the term virtual reality) teamed with Thomas Zimmerman to create a re-engineered version of VR that allowed users to communicate with the computer through a data glove. The data glove, when used by the viewer in conjunction with a head-mounted-display, served as a general-purpose interaction device that allowed the user to actually control certain features of the virtual environment. As VR viewing systems improved through research and development and the concept expanded to include interactivity, virtual environments could be used to compose like other artistic media, opening up entirely new continents of ideas and possibilities.

In a development parallel to the invention and refinement of HMD display systems, other forms of VR viewing were being investigated that employed different technological approaches to bringing the audience inside a computer image.

Facing page: From A *Volume of Two Dimensional Julia Sets* (1990), a computer animated 35mm stereoscopic film by Dan Sandin and associates. Sound by Laurie Spiegel.

Media artist Myron Krueger, a pioneer in the development of virtual environments, combined computers and video systems to create a new kind of immersive experience that he termed artificial reality. Krueger's aim was to use computers to establish a natural relationship between people and machines. The computer, in effect, would be taught about people instead of people having to learn about computers. In his best known installation work, *Videoplace* (initiated in the mid-1970s), Krueger created a framework for developing a series of ongoing demonstrations that allowed viewers to enter a dark room, face a large screen, and immediately start interacting with rear-projected computer-generated images. A visitor's body movements, when captured in real time by a video camera connected to a computer, basically determined what he or she would perceive. Essentially, the projected imagery of *Videoplace* consisted of the participants' colored silhouettes, allowing people to focus entirely on their interactions and experiences, not on the equipment itself. In essence, then, the viewers watched themselves as they were projected into a virtual world. Krueger also enhanced the experience of the participants by employing additional effects; for example, users could finger paint colored designs, send messages to each other and in one particular version called *Critter*, interact with a small animated graphic creature that was imbued with artificial intelligence. Although visitors to *Videoplace* were immersed in the imagery and could interact with it in various ways, it is important to note that the installation's formal parameters were conceived and programmed by the artist.

Another effective form of virtual reality that has been developed is the CAVE (a self-referential term, CAVE stands for Computer Automatic Virtual Environment). Invented by artist and technical innovator Dan Sandin and his associate Tom DeFanti in 1990, the classic CAVE is a three-sided room with stereographic imagery projected onto the walls and floor. Stereo spectacles are worn to experience the full 3D spatial effect. Several visitors can enter a CAVE together, although only one person using a hand-held interface device is able to actually interact with the imagery and see a perspective calculated from his or her point of view. Other individuals see the tracked imagery from a slightly oblique perspective. The CAVE is a totally immersive experience, a dynamic virtual environment that makes viewers feel as if they are in newly created time and space.

In addition to designing the CAVE, Sandin has also developed a number of other important electronic instruments, most notably the Sandin Image Processor (1973), a highly programmable analog computer for processing video images in real-time. Moreover, he has used these different instruments to produce a beautiful and prodigious body of artworks that have been exhibited widely both in America and abroad. In an interview that appears in this chapter, Sandin discusses in detail his VR installation works including *Poverty Island with Video Skies* (1998) and *Death's Door to the Garden Peninsula* (1999), as well as important technical and artistic achievements that preceded these projects. Indeed, it was his earlier excursions into image processing and computer-based autostereograms (PHSColograms) that prepared him for his innovative work with VR technology. By 1990 Sandin and DeFanti had formulated their CAVE concept and within two years they had developed a fully operational VR system capable of interactive three-dimensional displays of time-based imagery. Although the CAVE used a different viewing method from the head-mounted display approach, it initially employed the same type of imaging technique, namely, stereoscopic 3D computer

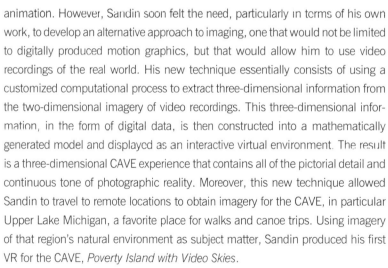

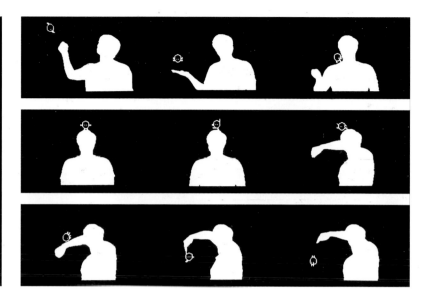

animation. However, Sandin soon felt the need, particularly in terms of his own work, to develop an alternative approach to imaging, one that would not be limited to digitally produced motion graphics, but that would allow him to use video recordings of the real world. His new technique essentially consists of using a customized computational process to extract three-dimensional information from the two-dimensional imagery of video recordings. This three-dimensional information, in the form of digital data, is then constructed into a mathematically generated model and displayed as an interactive virtual environment. The result is a three-dimensional CAVE experience that contains all of the pictorial detail and continuous tone of photographic reality. Moreover, this new technique allowed Sandin to travel to remote locations to obtain imagery for the CAVE, in particular Upper Lake Michigan, a favorite place for walks and canoe trips. Using imagery of that region's natural environment as subject matter, Sandin produced his first VR for the CAVE, *Poverty Island with Video Skies*.

From Death's Door to the Garden Peninsula, which was produced the following year, incorporated *Poverty Island with Video Skies* as one of its four major scenes. All the video for this piece was derived from panoramic views of nature shot in areas around Upper Lake Michigan. Three of the scenes are of islands, including Poverty Island, and one is of the Upper Peninsula. Once immersed in the imagery of *From Death's Door to the Garden Peninsula*, a viewer can navigate the CAVE's virtual environment by using a specially designed hand-held interface called a wand. For example, by pointing the wand at one of the four scenes and pushing a button a viewer experiences the sensation of moving toward that section of the imagery. As a viewer enters the selected scene it converts

into a panoramic image that fully envelops the CAVE. Two fixed cycles of time-lapsed imagery are then displayed followed by a third and final cycle during which a viewer can use the Wand to interactively colorize the scene in various ways. The three sequences conclude with an interactive computer-simulated scene of a luminescent waterfall. Composer Laurie Spiegel created electronic surround sound for the piece and Sandin produced real-time computer-generated sound effects.

Other artists who discuss their VR works in this chapter include Char Davies, Rebecca Allen and Michael Scroggins. Formerly a painter, Char Davies started working with 3D digital media in the late 1980s when she sought out time-based and spatial imaging techniques as an alternative to creating still images on a flat surface. Initially, a representational artist, Davies began in the early 1980s to paint in a more atmospheric style, layering images that were transparent, luminous and devoid of discreet shapes and resolute borders. She felt a need to alter her approach, to explore the expressive possibilities of pure light and to produce an expanded and poetic spatial experience. It was a creative impulse that could not be fully realized on the two-dimensional surface of a canvas and soon led to the investigation of new digital imaging methods that were emerging at that time. Setting aside her career as a painter Davies joined Montreal's Softimage, a fledgling start-up software company in its first year of operation. Within a short period of time she became a founding director of the company, a fast growing enterprise that produced the first software capable of creating 3D digital graphics without intense programming. As Softimage expanded, Davies stepped into a new role at the company that allowed her to once again focus on the development of her

technology. This new generation, on the other hand, thought they could take the original approach to another level by combining advanced electronic technology with industrial design, photography and perhaps the moving image, to produce a cybernetic revolution in the fields of art and design. And, of course, that's precisely what happened. However, it took twenty years or so before it became obvious to most people that this was going to transform the way we did business. During those early years the work that Tom DeFanti and I did with GRASS and the Image Processor was an integral part of this new direction and extremely critical to its development. Using our imaging systems in conjunction with a wide range of production techniques, we did a number of recorded video pieces that developed out of a whole series of performances we had done throughout the 1970s. The final piece in this evolving work was a videotape called *Spiral 5 PTL* (1980), and it became part of the inaugural collection of video art at the Museum of Modern Art in New York.

Q: Was dance integrated into *Spiral 5 PTL*?

DS: Yes, there was videotape of dance mixed into the piece, but the recorded performances of *Spiral* 1–3 did not include live dance. We did do live dance in conjunction with video in another series of pieces, but those performances were not part of the *Spiral* series.

Q: At this point you were still basically working with analog processes. When did you begin to work with digital media?

DS: It goes back a long way. I was, of course, working with digital computer graphics in the late 1960s when I was involved with physics, so it wouldn't be correct to say that I did the analog work first and then moved into digital imaging. I was, in fact, doing both digital and analog work all along, although there was a period during the 1970s when most of my work was concerned with analog processing.

By the end of the seventies analog calligraphic displays, which emerged in the 1960s, became technically outmoded and hard to maintain. Frame buffers were coming in at that time so people were capable of producing more naturalistic and photorealistic effects, as opposed to calligraphic imagery that consisted of bright lines on a dark screen that could be colored in various ways. As a result, our hybrid computer graphics system had to be put to sleep. Despite the emerging advances in digital technology, the new computer graphics, except for video games, basically could not move in real-time. Things had to be produced using

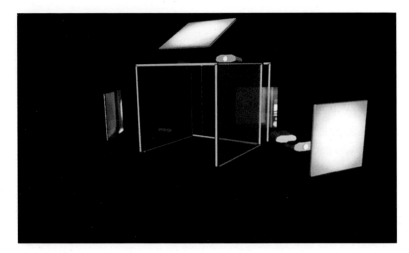

frame-by-frame animation techniques and it took a half hour or so per frame to compute and output a single image to film. I did a piece called *A Volume of Two Dimensional Julia Sets* using this digital animation technique and it was shown in stereo at Siggraph in 1991. I did another animation piece that was longer and more complicated in the 1980s, but it was not what I really wanted to do. My main interest, as it always has been, was to do live and interactive pieces. So Tom and I started to work with Bally Arcade video game technology and we developed a device called the Datamax UV-1 Zgrass. It was essentially a digital computer graphics system, but because it contained video game technology it could actually do a modest amount of stuff that was very close to real time. The Datamax UV-1 Zgrass gave us a more practical way to generate animation than the extremely time consuming frame-by-frame computer rendering technique that was being used at that time. Unlike other computers of the period, our machine was configured to ensure high quality NTSC video output.

There is another thread that should be mentioned regarding my work with digital computers that dates back to the late 1960s. At that time there was a device called the Link computer (Laboratory Instrument Computer) that was really a precursor of the modern personal computer. I used that digital computer in a collaborative project with Jerry Erdman and Myron Kruger. Kruger, by the way, began his pioneering work in the field of artificial reality about a year later. Anyway the piece, which was called *Glow Flow*, was a live interactive computer-controlled light and sound environment. The Link computer, which became the PDP-12, was quite amazing in that it had a full screen editor and it could do things in real-time. It not only processed visual data and managed the interactive features of the environment, but it also had ways of affecting the sound in the gallery space by running a Moog model 2 audio synthesizer. *Glow Flow* was completed in 1968

and shortly after traveled to the Smithsonian where it was exhibited for a period of time.

Q: At what point did you develop the CAVE and conceptually how did it evolve?

DS: The CAVE, in part, grew out of my interest in stereo (spatial imaging) that started back in the 1970s. Stereo has long fascinated me even though I have one-eyed vision and can't actually see stereo. In the mid-1980s I began working with Ellen Sandor to develop PHSCologram technology, a form of static stereo that can be viewed without glasses. It's essentially an autostereo process. She had developed a spatial imaging technique earlier that involved using a large press camera to record still lifes, but it had the same limitations as holography in the sense that you had to shoot objects that were placed on a tabletop. As a result, the process had certain limitations, but nevertheless she created a whole series of very interesting pieces using that approach. What I basically did was to fully computerize the process so that she could do digital things with the imagery instead of being limited essentially to photographic processes. As a result, both the technical quality and artistic range of this stereo technique were improved dramatically. Basically, I worked on the PHSCologram project with Ellen between 1986 and 1990 and she is still carrying on the work and doing a wonderful job.

Q: Your work with PHSColorgrams and 3D stereo imaging, then, helped prepare the way for developing the CAVE.

DS: Right, although there were actually a couple of connections that contributed

to the development of the CAVE. One is that the mathematics used to generate PHSColorgrams is exactly the same mathematics used to do projection based virtual reality. The other connection was that computers were able to generate moving images once again. I can remember when the predecessor to the personal Iris Silicon Graphics machine came out about 1987. I looked at the monitor and was very surprised to see animation. I had not seen this sort of imagery since the late 1970s when we put the GRASS machine together. It became clear then that the new computer technology was capable of doing much more than space roaches and video games, which moved, but had a very limited range of possibilities. I could imagine doing performance and interactive work on computers again. I began to focus on the possibilities of this new development and one of the concepts that interested me was virtual reality, which at the time was being done with head-mounted displays (HMD). So Tom and I decided to look into doing some art and scientific visualization using virtual reality, even though the resolution of HMD technology was very low and somewhat problematic. I don't know exactly how Tom and I came up with our alternative to the HMD, but I remember sitting around with him and talking about making some sort of virtual reality by surrounding our head with a number of big monitors. It took me just a few minutes to remember the work I did with PHSColorgrams and once that happened our idea quickly moved beyond the use of monitors to creating an environment with multiple projectors. So we hatched the CAVE concept somewhere around 1990. By July of 1992 we had developed a full-blown version of the CAVE and it was shown at Siggraph that year.

Q: Would you describe the general layout of the CAVE?

DS: The classic CAVE consists of three walls and a floor. The illusion of immersion is essentially created by projecting 3D computer graphics into a 10 ft. by 10 ft by 10 ft cube that surrounds the viewer. The graphics are coupled with a tracking system that produces the correct stereo perspective. The viewer explores the virtual world by physically moving around inside the cube and by manipulating the imagery using a three-button wand as an interface device. The original CAVE debuted at 1280 by 500 lines for each screen, which means it was 3600 lines around, a tremendous step in resolution quality compared to head-mounted displays – or any other computer display at that time. Once the CAVE was completed I was, of course, very interested in doing a virtual reality piece and immediately set out to make one for the Siggraph exhibition that year. I developed an interactive experience that involved simulated snowstorms. People visiting the CAVE could immerse themselves in these fields of moving particles and

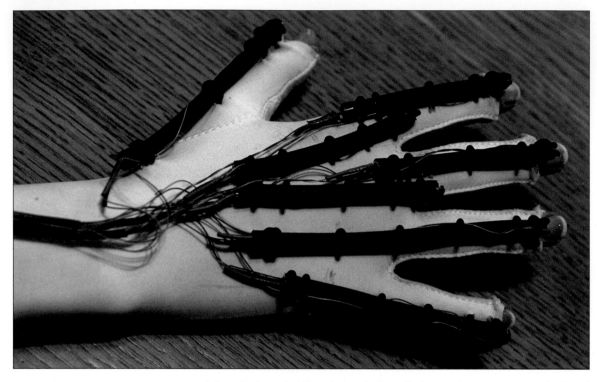

Above: The Sayre Glove was developed in 1976 by Dan Sandin and Tom DeFanti in association with Richard Sayre. A functioning prototype designed for use with the GRASS system, this "data glove" was the first input device of its kind. [© Dan Sandin.]

DS: Yes, it was definitely a first. Richard Sayre at the University of Chicago had the idea. We had the computer and I knew enough about electronic design to actually build the glove. I asked Rich for permission to make one so that we could try it out and he told us to go ahead. Tom and I built a functioning prototype, demonstrated it in public and wrote a report. It was actually funded as part of a project that involved developing radical input devices. At the time we did about ten different input devices that were very interesting. Our idea was to develop devices that were easier to use and better adapted to physical and human needs.

Q: Your CAVE installation, *Poverty Island with Video Skies* (1998), uses an unusual video technique to construct virtual reality. Would you discuss this piece?

SD: *Poverty Island with Video Skies* is a predecessor of a more recent work called, *From Death's Door to the Garden Peninsula* (1999). The two pieces, in a way, are connected to each other and basically consist of naturalistic imagery captured through video.

When I first started working with virtual reality, one of the things I found missing from my early video days was going out to these magnificent locations in Upper Lake Michigan, recording images of the natural environment, and then manipulating them into expressive pieces. In other words, virtual reality at that time could not incorporate camera images and had to be produced entirely with 3D computer generated graphics. Objects, as a result, often had a tendency to look like Fisher Price toys. I know that's an exaggeration and I don't mean to denigrate some really fine work that's been produced along those lines, but that's the tension I felt. In any case, I started to work on technology that would incorporate naturalistic images into an interactive virtual environment. When we first started using the CAVE there were a lot of people who would typically say things like, "I plan to take a video camera outside, videotape a space and then put it into the CAVE as a virtual reality piece". Of course, that wasn't possible because the conventional process of taking pictures is something that throws away the third dimension – or a real perception of space – and virtual reality is a deeply three dimensional medium. However, because of a tremendous amount of research that began in the early 1990s, it's now possible to videotape a subject, extract the three dimensional information from the imagery, use this information to construct a model, then display it as an interactive virtual environment.

interactively control the wind and other effects, creating a very atmospheric and kinetic virtual environment. Following Siggraph we had a number of other exhibitions that included mainly trade shows such as the NAB (National Association of Broadcasters) and the American Society of Radiology, for instance. We would exhibit examples of scientific visualization along with our art pieces.

Q: The interface for the CAVE is a hand-held wand, but earlier you had also done some pioneering work with other types of input devices including a data glove. Would you provide some background about these developments?

DS: In 1976 Tom Defanti and I developed what is now called the data glove and it looked a lot like the one that is in general use today. It was employed in combination with our real-time GRASS machine to basically produce certain kinds of gestural effects, not in the sense of gestural recognition, but more in the sense of gestural drawing where you could do complex expressive things with all the joints in your fingers. However, we only used it for a short time because it was developed when the GRASS machine was nearing the end of its lifetime.

Q: Was that a first?

Q: How did *Poverty Island with Video Skies* and *From Death's Door to the Garden Peninsula* evolve in terms of form and content?

DS: The panoramagram, *Poverty Island with Video Skies*, was produced first, then essentially the same location and imagery were shot on video again at a higher resolution and incorporated into *Death's Door* as one of the four major scenes. All of the imagery for both of these virtual reality works was recorded in areas around upper Lake Michigan.

Regarding form and content, *From Death's Door to the Garden Peninsula* consists basically of scenes from four different locations. Three of the scenes are of islands, including Poverty Island, and one is of the Upper Peninsula. In the CAVE, each of these places is displayed as a panoramagram and is accompanied by three other related images. So in a sense there are really twelve scenes in the piece, four separate panoramagrams each followed in sequence by two views of landscape detail and ending with a computer-simulated waterfall.

Q: How does the CAVE function as a virtual reality system?

DS: Essentially all virtual reality works the same way, whether it involves models generated mathematically, or models generated using a modeler or, in my case, models extracted from nature. It's also important to understand that virtual reality systems are quite independent of the processes that are used to actually construct these 3D models.

In terms of its technical and perceptual characteristics there are basically four pillars that extend virtual reality beyond conventional computer display technology. One of them is real-time interactivity. There are, of course, non-virtual reality displays like video games, that have this feature, but they lack the other three essential components. One of these other components is stereo. When viewing stereo you see things with both eyes and therefore experience the illusion of real depth. Another is surround viewing or immersion, meaning the artwork is not contained within a frame like painting, photography or video. In a sense, you view things from inside the scene. The fourth component is viewer-centered perspective, which has always struck me as the most amazing characteristic of all and really redefines what perspective means. For example, the traditional kinds of linear perspective found in renaissance painting or photography and video, is seen from a single point of view. In virtual reality the computer measures your position in space and creates a perspective from the viewer's point of view. So technically, it means that you can walk around and see the side, the top and the bottom of things by changing your point of view just like you do in the real world. This viewer-centered perspective, which is the first redefinition of perspective since the renaissance, is to me the most interesting thing about virtual reality and a thing I won't give up. I don't mean to say that you need all of these different properties to have a virtual reality system, but I think these are the kind of components required for an entirely new kind of visual medium.

Left: Frames from *Poverty Island with Video Skies* (1998), a virtual reality installation by Dan Sandin. Visitors to this interactive immersive work were able to vary the colorization of the image with a hand-held interface device.
[© Dan Sandin.]

Above: A single frame from a 360 degree time-lapse motion picture produced by Dan Sandin for his VR installation, *From Death's Door to the Garden Peninsula* (1999).
[© Dan Sandin.]

Q: Specifically, how is the stereo effect produced in the CAVE and how does it differ from stereo motion pictures?

DS: The CAVE supports stereo by essentially creating alternate projections for the left and right eyes. These alternate projections are viewed with shutter glasses that synchronously switch from transparent to opaque. As a result the left eye only sees the left image and the right eye only sees the right image. It's called frame sequential stereo and it's one of the two major elements needed to create virtual reality in the CAVE. The second major element has to do with head tracking or viewer-centered perspective. As you physically move around in the CAVE, the computer knows where you are located in space; it knows whether you're in the center of the CAVE, to one side, or somewhere else. By tracking your movement in the physical CAVE, the computer calculates your perspective on the virtual world. This tracking process essentially tells the computer where your two eyeballs are in the space. That's actually different from a theatrically released stereo motion picture in which the stereo effect is based on where the dual cameras were positioned during filming and has nothing to do with your location as a viewer. Therefore the stereo in the CAVE ends up being spatially much better than a stereo film because it's actually calculating what is seen from the position of the viewer's eyes.

Q: Once a viewer enters the CAVE and is immersed in *From Death's Door to the Garden Peninsula*, what kind of interactivity takes place?

DS: When you come into the CAVE you are surrounded by a cylindrical panoram-

agram that is cut up into four pie-shaped sections representing four places – Summer Island, Poverty Island, Rock Island and the Garden Peninsula. You navigate the virtual environment using a specially designed wand as an interface. By pointing the wand in the direction you want to go and pushing a button, you can move toward one of these places. When you enter the selected pie-shaped section it converts into a full panoramic version of that particular scene. At that point the scene – for example Poverty Island – changes from sunrise to sunset and you see the movement of the clouds, the water and so on. The first cycle through the sunrise and sunset is naturalistic. As you cycle through a second time you see a fixed colorized composition that I've produced for the piece. The third and final cycle can be controlled interactively by the viewer. For example, by moving the wand around and pushing the wand's joystick, the viewer can actually colorize the scene in different ways. However, most viewers don't realize they are using this feature because they are just too involved with what's generally happening. They tend to interact chiefly by navigating around the scene which is quite dramatic and which occupies most of their attention. When a scene finishes after about three minutes or so, you enter two 3D details of the scene in succession and then the sequence ends with a computer-simulated waterfall. At that point, if you have time, you can go back to the beginning and select another scene.

Q: Laurie Spiegel composed the sound for the *Poverty Island* piece. Did she also compose the sound for *From Death's Door to the Garden Peninsula*?

DS: Much of the same sound that was used in *Poverty Island* was also used in *Death's Door*. Laurie Spiegel and I have worked together on a number of pieces over the years and we have had several different kinds of working relationships. In the case of these virtual reality works, I sent her videotapes and some still images of the imagery I was working on and she, in turn, selected some music that she had previously composed and that she thought would be appropriate.

She then sent me that music and I incorporated it into *Poverty Island* and later into *Death's Door*. Another audio component of *Death's Door* consisted of real time and algorithmic sound effects that I generated and blended with Laurie's compositional work.

Q: How exactly does the sound relate to the interactive environment of *From Death's Door to the Garden Peninsula*?

DS: The sound, in a sense, is like a series of theme songs. What you hear depends on where you are in the piece. Each scene has different music and sound effects associated with it. However, in the third section of each scene, when you move from the 3D reconstructed details of these beautiful islands in northern Lake Michigan and enter a waterfall environment, the sound is algorithmically generated and relates directly to the simulated physics of water falling in virtual space. By processing samples of white noise I produced other sorts of noise that were blended together in real time so that as you enter the stream of water it sounds like it's falling on you, or falling near you, or bouncing off the wand that you're holding in your hand. In addition, one of Laurie's compositions is playing in the background. As an interactive experience it's quite effective. In my next work I'm actually going to combine these water effects with 3D models so that they can occur within the context of natural scenes from upper Lake Michigan.

Q: All of your recent artistic projects have involved some sort of artistic collaboration with artists and scientists. How would you describe your relationship with these individuals? Was it a hiearchial arrangement or a more interactive type of relationship?

DS: All of this work that I've talked about is really the product of a community made up of artists and scientists operating here at the University of Illinois at Chicago. We began as the Circle Graphics Habitat in 1973 and changed our name to the Electronic Visualization Lab in 1980. It's a large and ever changing community that's been working on the development of new media over a period of many years. For example, the invention of the CAVE and the success of the virtual reality pieces in the CAVE come from this working environment as much as they do from individuals.

The model for our type of collaboration is more interactive than hierarchical.

Upper image: Dan Sandin in the CAVE theatre interacting with a digitally simulated waterfall, an animated effect he created for his virtual reality installation. From *Death's Door to the Garden Peninsula* (1999). [© Dan Sandin.]

Lower image: An image from *From Death's Door to the Garden Peninsula* (1999), a virtual reality installation by Dan Sandin. [© Dan Sandin.]

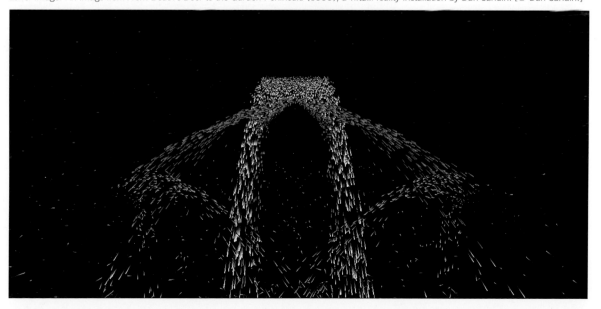

Left: From A *Volume of Two Dimensional Julia Sets* (1990), a computer animated 35mm stereoscopic film by Dan Sandin and associates. Sound by Laurie Spiegel.

For instance, in some cases the scientists would properly be called the artistic directors of a work because the project is essentially driven by their ideas and sense of vision. In other cases the process consists of the artists working essentially on their own, but getting help from scientists to write some piece of code or to understand certain classes of technical problems. Growth in this field is dependent upon all kinds of practical and imaginative approaches to collaboration.

In particular, we are interested in teaching artists enough about technology so that they can either operate independently or they can have effective collaborative relationships with scientists. However, a lot of this educational process involves scientists helping the artists to understand how to do their work. There are those in the field who have a different viewpoint and feel that we need to develop renaissance teams of artists and scientists to generate good forms of visualization. I'm not interested in renaissance teams: I'm interested in renaissance people. ✧

From an audiotape interview, February 2002.

Char Davies

Formally a painter and filmmaker, Char Davies began working with digital media in the late 1980s. Her 3D computer-generated still images, collectively known as *The Interior Body Series*, took the form of light boxes, beautiful translucent images that immediately received international recognition for their extraordinary graphics and advanced use of software. In the mid-1990s, seeking to further expand her expressive capabilities through digital technology, Davies abandoned the two-dimensional picture plane of her luminous still images and began to explore the multi-dimensional realm of virtual reality. In her interactive VR works, *Osmose* (1995) and *Ephémère* (1998), Davies avoids the standard practices of virtual reality and pursues an alternative approach, an avenue of spatial imaging that not only complements her own personal sense of vision, but also suggests new possibilities for the evolution of the medium. Her VR works, for example, are not addressed through the ordinary hand-based mode of user-interaction, but rather embody an interface that tracks breath and shifting balance, grounding the immersive experience in the participant's own body. Moreover, her works circumvent the solid hard-edged realism toward which most VR works aspire and instead rely on semi-abstract, semi-transparent imagery to create ambiguous but evocative effects which actively engages the participant's imagination. Her poetic and enveloping environments, which are derived from the natural world and its underlying processes, seek to explore the more contemplative and reflective potential of virtual reality.

Born in Toronto, Canada in 1954, Davies studied fine arts at Bennington College, Vermont, and received a visual arts degree at the University of Victoria in British Columbia in 1978. For the next ten years she worked as a painter and as an independent director for the National Film Board of Canada. In 1987 Davies joined Softimage, a Canadian based software company, to work in the areas of 3D computer graphics and animation. She left Softimage in 1997 and formed Immersence Inc. as a vehicle for pursuing her artistic research in the field of virtual reality.

Her immersive environments, *Osmose* and *Ephémère* have been exhibited in Montreal, New York, London and Monterrey, Mexico among other cities. In addition to her artistic activities, Davies has published numerous papers about her work and lectured widely at museums, cultural institutions and conferences including The Doors of Perception in Amsterdam, Siggraph and the Museum of Modern Art in New York.

Interview with CHAR DAVIES

Q: You were educated in the arts and began your career as a painter. Would you discuss your transition from painting to computer graphics and specifically what attracted you to this new medium?

Char Davies: My research in computer graphics and VR is rooted in the years I worked as a painter. During that time I produced a body of work that was concerned with the intermingling of the interior self and the exterior world, the conjoining of body and nature. To visually achieve this synthesis, I developed an approach to painting in which multiple levels of luminous semitransparent forms were employed to create varying degree of perceptual ambiguity. These paintings were dense and complex works, composed of semi-abstract imagery related to landscape.

I abandoned painting in 1987 because of the inherent limitations of the two-dimensional picture plane. As my ideas about form and content developed, I felt the need to explore new and more expansive ways of imaging. Consequently, I eventually began investigating three-dimensional computer-based techniques that were capable of communicating a multisensory experience involving spatial envelopment and the passage of time. Painting, nevertheless, was a very important stage in my development as an artist and provided the conceptual basis for my later work with digital media.

During my formative years as a painter, I concentrated on mastering classical drawing and painting techniques. I wanted to learn the rules of representation

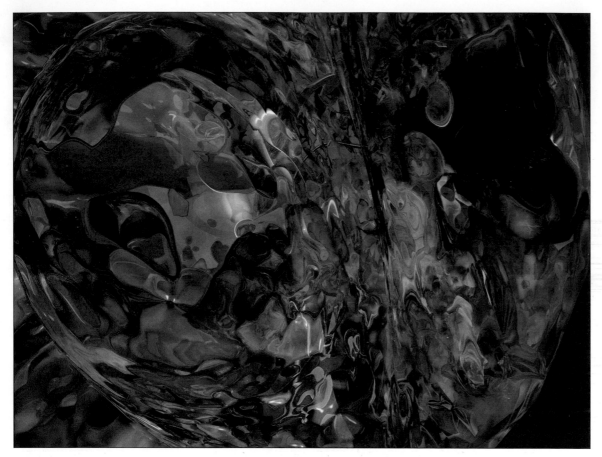

Above: Stream (1991), from *The Interior Body Series* by Char Davies. During the early 1990s Char Davies made a series of still computer-generated images, which were produced by creating 3D models in virtual space and then moving the computer's virtual camera to capture the desired framing. Each of these images was displayed as a large transparency in the form of a light box.
[© Immersance.]

observed, between the interior self and the exterior world. This mode of perceptual spatiality, one in which the body feels the envelopment of space much like that of a body immersed in the sea, has become an integral part of my work.

The limitations of painting's two-dimensional picture plane for representing light in flux and three-dimensional space became increasingly apparent to me, as did the medium's limited capacity for suggesting envelopment within that space. I began looking for a more effective means of visualization. Around 1982, I saw a very early example of 3D computer graphics, an animated film called *Vol de Rêve*. It consisted of a character throwing ping-pong balls into a pond. The imagery was made with vector graphics, phosphorescent green lines against an empty black space. When I saw this piece, I intuitively knew that the technique of 3D computer graphics might well prove to be the medium I was seeking. What attracted me were not the graphics, but the three-dimensionality of the space, specifically the working space.

The desire to work in such a space led me on a bit of a detour in terms of my work as an artist, namely that of building the 3D software company, Softimage. I became a founding director in early 1988. As the company grew and our programming team developed 3D software tools, I began making experimental still images. Unfortunately, no traces of these earliest CG (computer graphics) works remain because there was no renderer in the infant software at that time and, therefore, no way to save images. The first rendered image I produced, a stylized atmospheric work entitled *Leaf*, won an Ars Electronica Award in 1990. This image was a still frame of a three-dimensional scene in which very simple voluminous forms were mapped with semitransparent textures to create implied complexity due to the casting of light and shadow within the scene. One of the textures, as I recall, was from a scanned medical photo of arteries in the human brain. *Leaf* was followed by an image entitled *Blooming (Vessel)*, which was intended to evoke the veiny interior of a flower in the process of blooming as well as a sense of body flesh. These two works led to *Root* (1991), an image that alluded to both a root in subterranean soil and to an umbilical cord in the womb. Other works that were part of what I termed *The Interior Body Series* included *Drowning (Rapture)* and *Yearning*, a still image that received an Ars Electronica Distinction in 1993. All of these images dealt with the metaphor of co-equivalence between the subjective interior body and elements found in nature. They were produced by working with extremely simple 3D forms and very complex 3D lighting effects. However, while each image was captured from a 3D virtual scene, the end result, in terms of output medium, remained two-dimensional. These pieces were exhibited as large-scale transparencies in the form of light boxes and were experienced by the viewing public as flat 2D static images. Once again, I

before I broke them. Gradually I became more and more interested in light rather than form, to the point where I was making paintings of glass jars set on mirrors. In these studies, form became transparent and all that remained were reflections and refractions of light in space. During this phase of my work, I was influenced by the extreme myopic condition of my own eyesight, a condition that transforms all hard edges and the surfaces of things, dissolving objects into soft, semi-transparent, ambiguous, volumes of varying hue and luminosity.

In 1985 I made a painting that was very important to me relative to my work with immersive environments. This painting dealt with landscape, yet all reference to form was absent, leaving only light in flux in three-dimensional space. I continued to explore this direction and began producing paintings that were about the sensation of being in the landscape, not in terms of its surface appearances, but in terms of being encircled by a horizon, immersed in flowing light and enveloped by nature's processes. I was concerned with manifesting a type of spatiality in which there is a porous boundary between the observer and the felt the medium I was using was incapable of conveying what I wanted to communicate.

By early 1993, I began to consider VR as a potentially more capable medium. What interested me about VR, at the time, was not its interactive capacity, but rather its enveloping spatial quality that allowed viewers, hitherto kept outside of the imagery, to become participants, virtually crossing over to the other side of the 2D picture plane into an enveloping 3D space. After spending six months conceptualizing such a VR project, I put together a team and we proceeded to construct *Osmose*.

Q: How would you describe *Osmose* (1995) in terms of its equipment, software and physical layout?

CD: To experience *Osmose*, the participant or immersant, dons a stereoscopic helmet (head-mounted display) through which the computer-generated 3D graphics and 3D sound are experienced in real-time. The immersant interacts with the graphics and sound by controlling his or her rate of breathing and center of balance. These physical actions and responses are tracked by sensors mounted on a vest worn by the immersant, and then transmitted to customized software that resides in a computer. There's no data glove, joystick or other conventional device involved. The vest is the only physical interface used in the process.

During public exhibitions the immersant, wearing a head-mounted display and the specially designed vest, is placed in a small private chamber. The chamber faces onto a large darkened audience space that has two projection screens. This public space is filled with sound that is generated in real-time by the immersant's behavior in the virtual space. One of the screens displays a stereoscopic video projection of the 3D world being experienced by the immersant. This projection enables the audience to vicariously witness each phase of the virtual journey as it takes place in real-time. The other screen displays the projected shadow of the immersent's silhouette as he or she moves and gestures in response to the work. The use of this shadow-silhouette, alongside the real-time video projection, serves to poeticize the relationship between the immersant's body and the work, drawing attention to the body's role as a medium for the interactive experience.

Q: What does the word *Osmose* mean?

CD: *Osmose* is a French term for osmosis and it refers to a biological process involving passage from one side of a membrane to another. Osmosis can also be thought of as a metaphor for achieving transcendence through the dissolution of

boundaries between the inner and the outer: in other words, the inter-mingling of self and world. It was in this sense that I conceived and developed the form and content of *Osmose*. As an artwork it was motivated by a desire to heal the Cartesian split between mind and body, subject and object, that has shaped our cultural values and contributed to our estrangement from life. In effect, then, *Osmose* is designed to increase ones sensitivity and to create a heightened awareness of ones own existence by *deautomatizing* habitual perceptions.

Q: How is the virtual space within *Osmose* structured?

CD: There are twelve virtual world-spaces within *Osmose*. Most of these, with the exception of an introductory Cartesian Grid, are based on symbolic elements in nature that have been developed over 25 years in my work. Among the world-spaces are *Forest*, *Leaf*, *Clearing*, *Pond*, *Abyss*, *Tree*, *Earth* and *Cloud*. Two

Above: Clearing with tree and pond: a real-time frame capture from Char Davies' VR installation *Osmose* (1995). In this immersive work, the participant experiences the symbolic realms of twelve different universes: forest, clearing, stream, leaf, pond, earth, etc. Based on a real-time body centered experience, the piece strives to dissolve the boundaries between self and nature.
[© Immersance.]

Right: An installation view of *Osmose* (1995), an interactive virtual environment by Char Davies. This VR work utilizes stereoscopic 3D computer animation and spatial sound, which is activated in real-time. The participant wears a stereoscopic head-mounted display and a "motion capture" vest with a breathing and balance sensor to enter the environment. Sound is also affected by bodily movement. Multiple viewers can see the environment through stereo glasses, but only one person (the immersant) can have the total VR experience.
[© Immersance.]

other world-spaces include *Code*, which contains lines of the custom software used to create the work, and *Text*, which contains excerpts of relevant philosophical and poetic texts about nature, the body and technology. *Code* and *Text* function as conceptual substratum and superstratum and bracket the work. All of these world-spaces connect to one another in various ways. There is also a space called *Lifeworld* that appears at the end when it is time to bring an immersive session to a close.

Q: Would you discuss the production process used to plan and build *Osmose*, and your second VR piece *Ephémère* (1998)? For example, do you have some sort of system for storyboarding or diagramming your VR works and their interactive features, or do you basically improvise as the work develops?

CD: While assembling the team for *Osmose* in the Spring of 1994, I wrote a mission statement for the company (Softimage, Inc.) stating that the objective of my research was to explore the expressive capabilities of VR and thereby demonstrate that it was capable of producing serious works of art. As such, *Osmose* was conceived as an alternative to mainstream VR that, at the time, consisted primarily of shoot 'em up games and architectural flythroughs. Six months prior to hiring my production team, I began writing a twenty plus page document in which I outlined many of the goals of the project in terms of content, interactivity and aesthetics. As yet, I have declined to publish this particular paper because some of the ideas in it are yet to be realized and will go into a third or even fourth work. This "white paper", which outlined my plan in detail, acted as our touchstone for developing the project.

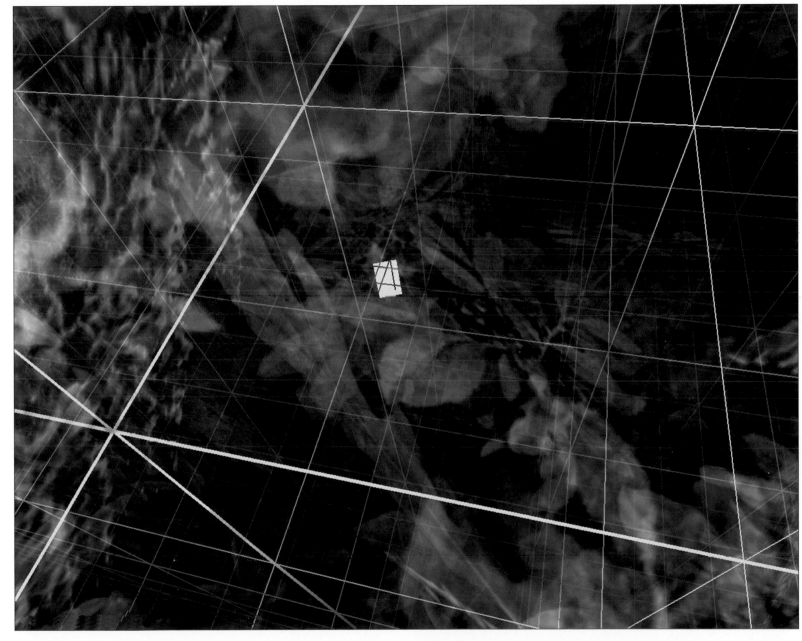

Left: Cartesian grid and forest, a real-time frame capture from Char Davies' VR installation *Osmose* (1995).
[© Immersance.]

The core team for both *Osmose* and *Ephémère* consisted of John Harrison, who did all the custom programming and Georges Mauro, who built the models, added the textures and worked out the animations using the Softimage software. Both John and Georges were familiar with my previous work and aesthetic through my earlier drawings and paintings, and in particular *The Interior Body Series*. In addition Georges and I had previously worked together on the CG-animated film, *West of Eden* in the late 1980s at Softimage. During that time Georges had an opportunity to become familiar with my visual approach and sensibility. I was fortunate to have a team that trusted me and respected my vision as an artist. It was a relationship that contributed immensely to the creative process.

Right: Subterranean world with rocks, root systems and a stream, a real-time frame capture from Char Davies' VR installation *Osmose* (1995).
[© Immersance.]

Below: Seeds, a real-time frame capture from *Ephémère* (1998), a VR installation by Char Davies. Like *Osmose*, *Ephémère* is based on natural worlds but it employs a different spatial concept, a vertical structure consisting of three distinct levels: landscape, subterranean earth and interior body. It also introduces new interactive features and an expanded temporal layer consisting of various life cycles as well as daily and seasonal changes.
[© Immersance.]

Generally, I tend to use an improvised approach to my work, rather than executing and implementing a pre-planned concept or storyboard. In other words, I feel my way along, proceeding intuitively and responding to the work itself as it's created. In a way, it was the same method I used when painting, though developed much further. I filled many notebooks with ideas, lists, charts, schematics and rough sketches, and this was my way of keeping track of the project and working out various possibilities as we progressed. Sometimes I'd show these notes and drawings to the team, but usually I wouldn't. Decisions about how we would proceed were based on my intuitive response to the material we were creating at the time. This approach to the work allows for a great deal of exploration, but on the other hand it is far more time consuming than a straightforward production based on storyboards and pre-planned strategies. However, the advantage of using an improvised method is that the work always remains fresh and alive during the creative process.

Q: **At what point during the conceptual process do you begin making decisions about sound design?**

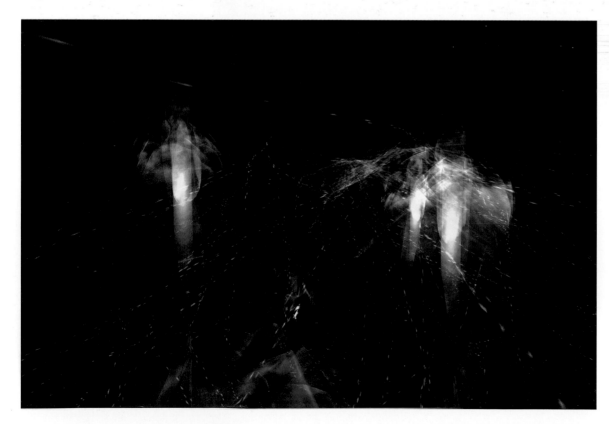

CD: Ideally, I would like to bring in a sound team and begin sound research as early as possible. In the case of *Osmose*, however, the team involved with the sound component of the piece joined us in the final three months of the project. Dorota Blaszczzch came from Poland to work as the sound engineer, placing all the sounds in three-dimensional space and working with the sounds' interactivity. "Sound engineer", however, is an inadequate term to describe her role. "Sonic architect" is perhaps a more appropriate title because of the sounds' complex spatial configuration. Musician Rick Bidlack joined us as composer. Rick and Dorota were also involved in the sound design of *Ephémère*. The production of sound, like the imagery, was very improvised and process-oriented.

Q: **How does your most recent VR work,** *Ephémère***, differ from** *Osmose***?**

CD: In *Ephémère*, the iconography extends beyond the trees, water and other

elements of the exterior natural world found in *Osmose*, to include body organs, blood vessels and bones, for example. These elements are intended to suggest a symbolic correspondence between the interior body and the subterranean earth, which was developed in my earlier work. While *Osmose*, on the one hand, consists of a dozen world-spaces, *Ephémère*, on the other, is structured spatially into three levels: landscape, subterranean earth and interior body. Unlike *Osmose*, *Ephémère* also has an ever-changing temporal structure. As the immersant roams among all three realms, no realm is static or remains the same. The environment at each level changes continuously, passing through cycles of dawn, day, evening and night, from the pale of winter through spring, summer, and then onto the climactic decay of autumn. While the participant may spend an entire session in one realm, it is more likely that he or she will pass among the various levels, immersed in an ongoing transformation of visual elements and sound. Subterranean rocks, roots, seeds and other natural elements, for example, come into being, linger and pass away. Their appearance depends on the immersant's *gaze*, as well as their rate of motion and location within the environment.

All the transformations and interactions in *Ephémère* are aural as well as visual. While the visual elements pass through varying phases of visibility and non-visibility, the sound is also in a continuous state of flux. Located in enveloping

3D space and fully interactive, the audio oscillates between melodic and mimetic effects[3] in a state somewhere between structure and chaos, adapting moment by moment to the spatiotemporal activity of the immersant.

Ephémère is also more interactive and transformative than *Osmose*. For example, seeds in the earth can be activated when *gazed* upon for an extended length of time, rewarding the immersant's patient observation with germination. *Ephémère*'s river, which has a gravitational pull, may morph into an underground stream, an artery or a vein once the immersant is within its flow. Rocks, deep within the earth may transform into pulsating body organs, eggs can appear and aging appendages can give way to bone. As these elements evolve and change, they are accompanied by corresponding aural transformations. Depending on the immersant's behavior while navigating within the work; there can be several possible endings.

The visuals in *Osmose* and *Ephémère* are soft, luminous and translucent, consisting of semi-transparent 3D forms. These 3D forms have been designed neither to be totally representational, nor completely abstract, but to hover somewhere in between. By animating these forms, and by enabling the participant not only to see through them, but to float through them bodily as well, it is possible to create spatially ambiguous effects and relationships. These sensory fluctuations

Above: Summer forest, a real-time frame capture from *Ephémère* (1998), a VR installation by Char Davies.
[© Immersance.]

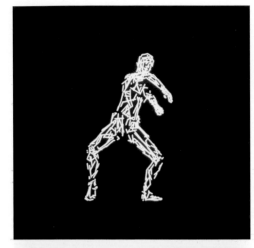

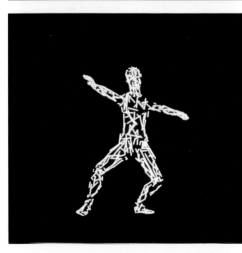

Rebecca Allen

A sense of the surreal, elegantly designed graphics and a concern for the dynamics of human movement suffuse the media works of Rebecca Allen. During her career, which spans more than twenty years, Allen has been at the forefront of the digital graphics movement as an artist and innovator. Building on her earlier works with computer animation and multimedia performance, Allen in recent years has focused on using the computer to develop immersive and interactive experiences. In an installation piece such as *The Bush Soul* (1997–2002), for example, Allen created a complex virtual world that allows viewers – through the use of avatars – to interact with a multisensory environment and the artificial life-forms that inhabit it. The boundary that traditionally exists between the viewer and the viewed is thereby dissolved, reality re-invented and, as a result, the installation becomes a medium for the exploration of a complex social environment and ultimately the examination of self. *The Bush Soul*, like other works by Allen such as *The Catherine Wheel* (1982), *Point of Departure* (1992) *and Coexistence* (2001), explore the new technical capabilities of media, integrating sound, image and motion in ways that alter the artistic parameters of time and space and introduce new aesthetic issues.

Allen attended the Rhode Island School of Design during the early 1970s where she was awarded a BFA in visual arts and began experimenting with animation. She continued her studies at the Massachusetts Institute of Technology, receiving an MS degree and becoming a member of the MIT Architecture Machine Group (now known as the Media Lab). Following her academic residency at MIT she became associated with the New York Institute of Technology where she was actively engaged in computer animation research and production for six years. She created a number of commissioned media works in both Europe and the United States and designed award-winning projects for the entertainment industry. Allen also

contributed to a number of intermedia performances, collaborating with Twyla Tharp, the Joffrey Ballet, La Fura dels Baus and Peter Gabriel. In 1993 she became a creative director and associate producer at Virgin Interactive Entertainment, a computer gaming company, and in 1996 became founding co-director of the Center for Digital Arts at the University of California at Los Angeles.

Awards include an Emmy for "outstanding individual achievement", and Japan's Nicograph Award for "artistic and technical excellence". Allen's media works, in addition to being exhibited internationally, reside in the permanent collections of numerous institutions including the Centre Georges Pompidou in Paris, the Ludwig Museum in Cologne and the Whitney Museum of Art in New York.

Excerpts from an interview with Erkki Huhtamo, 4 July 1999.

Erkki Huhtamo: How did you first get involved with computers, technology and art?

Rebecca Allen: I became interested in technology as an art student at Rhode Island School of Design (RISD) in the early 1970s. I studied the art and technology movements of the early twentieth century, such as the Bauhaus, the Futurists and the Constructivists. I was very interested in the idea of artists exploring the latest technology and trying to help society understand its relationship to technology. I was also intrigued by the idea of artists using new technology as a tool to create new art forms. As I began to think about the technologies of our time and their impact I recognized that computers would become an important part of society and could be important tools for artists as well.

In trying to push the boundaries of traditional art I became interested in the use of motion. Initially, I was studying graphic design – this was about 1972–73 – but I wasn't interested in static images: I wanted images to move, to come to life. My role models were not cartoon animators, but Duchamp and other artists who had experimented with motion in the early 1900s.

A few things at RISD really inspired me. One was a lecture and film showing by John Whitney Sr., a pioneer in computer graphics. I also had a professor, David Brisson, who talked about four-dimensional space. The idea of mathematics and multiple dimensions intrigued me. Then, in 1974, I saw a stereo computer-generated film that visualized four-dimensional rotations of hyper-cubes. It was made by Tom Banchoff and Charles Strauss, professors respectively in mathematics and computer science at Brown University, which was right next to RISD. This convinced me to explore the possibilities of computer animation.

EH: How did you come to use the computer yourself?

RA: I changed my field of study to film animation and video in order to explore the graphic aspect of motion ... I made up a course called *Computer Animation* that I proposed to RISD through Brown University. My RISD teachers were very sceptical about the idea, saying artists didn't need to work with this kind of technology, but they agreed to let me go ahead. So I began to work with a computer called a Vector General. It didn't have a frame buffer yet, so everything was drawn as vector lines – that was state of the art of computer animation then ... I created animation using graphs and punch cards – a keyboard interface didn't exist either. This was how I made my first computer animation in 1974.

EH: Can you describe what it was like?

RA: Actually, I still have the drawings from it. I was interested in the idea of computer rotoscoping, a technique where you digitize a live-action film, a frame at a time, and transform it into animated drawings. I used the natural movement of the human figure, but I abstracted and stylized the imagery through animated drawings. I somehow acquired a number of erotic films from the 1950s and transformed one of them that showed a woman lifting up her dress as she danced around. That was my first computer animation. I did it because I was struggling with the sense that the computer was anti-human. I wanted computer art to be something sensual and slightly erotic. This seemed the antithesis of what a computer was supposed to be.

EH: What happened next?

RA: After I graduated from art school, I worked as a graphic designer for a furniture design company, but it became clear to me that I didn't want to be a graphic designer. I really wanted to explore technology. I spent a good deal of time looking around for places where anything was going on with computer animation. I called the NYIT computer graphics lab – they had just started – also MIT's Lincoln Lab and Bell Labs where Ken Knowlton was working. I also knew about MIT's Architecture Machine Group (Arch Mach) and Ohio State University. There were so few places to go at that time.

I decided to attended MIT as a special student and enrolled in a course that was co-taught by Nicholas Negroponte. It was one of the very early computer graphics courses. A graduate program was being developed but it wasn't yet open for admissions. After completing the class, I continued to spend a lot of time in

the Arch Mach lab. In the meantime I applied for the graduate program and was accepted.

EH: What was your role at the Architecture Machine Group and what projects did you participate in?

RA: We were exploring ways to use interactive multimedia for education and training. This led to my thesis work, which involved the development of a system that transformed live-action film to stylized animation. The thesis was titled, *Computer Rotoscoping with the Aid of Color Recognition*. As you can see, I followed up on my earlier interest in art in motion.

EH: What was the impact of MIT and the Architecture Machine Group on your work?

RA: We explored the design of human-computer interfaces, and we used gesture control, voice recognition, eye tracking, speech synthesis and graphics. This turned me on to a number of new directions. It was an incredible learning experience about all the things that were possible with technology. I worked with

Above: From *Adventures in Success* (1983), an award-winning music video directed by Rebecca Allen. The video's imagery, designed and created by Allen, depicts modern symbols of success through a combination of 2- and 3D computer animation and live-action videography. Music by Will Powers, Robert Palmer and Sting. [Island Records.]

Facing page: Still frames from a computer wire-frame model by Rebecca Allen for Twyla Tharp's dance video, *The Catherine Wheel* (1982). In this work choreographed live dance is interspersed with Allen's three-dimensional digital model, a stylized depiction of Saint Catherine. When Allen designed this animated figure it represented one of the most intricate and advanced examples of 3D computer-generated human motion and was the first of its kind to be aired on television.

Sequence of three images: From *Laberint* (1992), a video short by Rebecca Allen. Based on the Platonic myth that woman and man were once one androgynous form, this work consists of live-action and computer-generated characters that weave between real and virtual worlds. Music by John Paul Jones [Opal Records.]

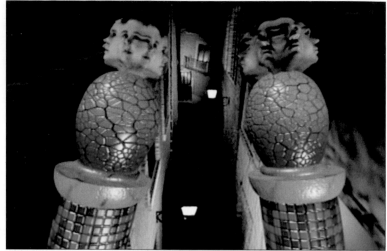

High Definition Studios to design a work on HDTV, and I created a piece called *Behave*. At that time the field of artificial life (A-life) was just emerging and a good friend of mine, Craig Reynolds, had developed beautiful flocking algorithms for flying 3D models. With artificial life software one could set up procedures based on simple rules that would bring computer models to life and they would behave in ways that appeared to be natural and familiar. I knew that A-life would become an important direction for my work so I proposed a project that would integrate live-action and 3D animation using Craig's A-life software.

EH: Around the end of the 1980s and early 90s you ended up creating several works in Spain. How did this happen?

RA: In L.A. I had met the Spanish artist and curator Montxo Algora, who was convinced that computer art was the future of art. When he founded Art Futura in Barcelona in 1990 he invited me to produce work for the festival. I had already created a piece called *Steady State* for a Spanish television series called *El Arte del Video*. Montxo suggested that I would work with *La Fura dels Baus*, a well-known performance group. I had expressed an interest in working with them after attending one of their performances – their work was very raw, physical and aggressive. While the audience stood throughout a large open space, *La Fura* appeared from all directions, performing to intense live music on fast moving mobile stages. Their strong physical presence expressed primal desires and was often combined with water, fire, food, animal entrails, blood, paint and explosions. The audience was forced to move and interact; this was the ultimate interactive three-dimensional experience.

La Fura dels Baus is a group of nine men, and our collaboration was the first time they had worked with a woman, so they decided this piece would be about women and include woman performers. We created a piece titled *Mugra* and experimented with ways to integrate electronic technology ... with their very raw heavy industrial kind of performance. We settled on placing seventy video monitors throughout the space that hung just above the audience's heads and were at times activated with pneumatic motors. I created a series of animated images that complemented the physical performance ... I was also commissioned to create three pieces for the opening of the Seville World Expo and segments of a large-scale live multimedia performance called *Memory Palace*.

For *Memory Palace* I designed a piece using the highest quality flight simulator. I was interested in virtual reality and real-time 3D graphics, but I wanted very high quality images, so I contacted a company in England called Redifusion, which was known to be one of the best flight simulator companies. Working with their flight simulator pilot I choreographed camera movements through simulations of different parts of the world. The edited film was presented across three giant screens. Being in a flight simulator is an incredible experience; you really experience the sense of movement. You can feel nauseous when things fly too fast or in the wrong direction. I wanted to give a large audience the sense of being in a simulator by projecting it as a large-scale panorama.

EH: Then came one of the most surprising moves of your career. You became a videogame developer.

RA: After completing work with the flight simulator, I wanted to pursue the idea

of real-time high resolution 3D virtual worlds, but I didn't want to continue negotiating the use of multimillion dollar machines. So I decided to enter the video game world. I wasn't a game player, but some of the coolest 3D technology was taking place in the video game industry. And there was my interest in pop culture – this was where young people were going; they lived in video games and quickly understood their interactive language. I wanted to learn more about interactive entertainment to understand better this side of pop culture while actually making games.

Many colleagues were surprised and disapproved of my move to a game company. The first game I completed was *Demolition Man*, based on the movie. I did something unusual for me: I created a violent shoot 'em up game. I was a misfit there, in one sense studying that culture but simultaneously participating in it. And after a couple of years I began to get tired of working with very difficult technology only to build commercial products.

EH: After you retreated from the game industry, what happened next?

RA: I was offered a position at the University of California (UCLA) as a professor and chair of a new department of design that was converting to digital media. This was good because it allowed me to get back to my artistic work.

EH: Now that you look back, is it possible for a computer artist to make an impact on culture?

RA: I'm a bit disappointed, because when I started back in the early 1970s, I was sure that within ten or fifteen years computer art would be in the forefront. I

also thought the art world would change and the idea of the single, original art object exhibited in a museum would go through radical changes. It is still not happening. I also thought that art created with new technology would be distributed in a way that is similar to music distribution – where you could purchase art through a variety of channels. Experimental music may not sell a large amount, but it is available in record stores. That hasn't happened to computer art, and may not happen soon. Yet I believe that in the future it will become obvious that the exploitation of digital media in art is very important and that certain important works have been created over the years and will finally be recognized.

Interview with REBECCA ALLEN

Q: When did you start working on your virtual reality installation, *The Bush Soul*?

Rebecca Allen: It began in the mid-1990s. I was able to get research funding from Intel to develop a new type of programming tool called Emergence. To help with the project, I enlisted a computer science and design team here at UCLA. The result was a real-time interactive software system, a behavior scripting language capable of supporting virtual 3D environments filled with A-life (artificial life) forms. These forms are able to communicate with each other and respond to a multitude of situations. Our software system was also designed to accommodate user interactivity, allowing a participant to navigate within virtual space and to affect the behavior of these A-life forms through a hand-held input device. As our software project developed it was coupled with my idea for an installation piece – *The Bush Soul* – and used to support its interactive world.

Although the Emergence project had certain practical objectives, it was also a way to use sponsored research to create new artworks. It's a strategy I've used to produce just about all my projects. I've been with computer labs, worked on prototype software, and participated in a variety of research projects, always with the intention of furthering my work and developing my own ideas and personal approach to imagery. My art, in a sense, is often disguised as research because I've found it's an effective way to acquire funding and technical support to do incredibly expensive kinds of animation. In the case of Intel, I think it's been a mutually beneficial arrangement. They've been satisfied with the technical aspects of my research and also quite happy to see me doing artwork that's exhibited and getting a lot of exposure.

Q: Is *The Bush Soul* a work-in-progress or has it been completed?

RA: Actually I've developed three versions of *The Bush Soul*. We're still making some small changes on the interactive component of the third and final version, but for all intents and purposes it's done. The piece evolved from a single screen work (which debuted in October of 1997 at Madrid's Art Futura Festival) into a version capable of supporting three wrap-around screens for a full immersion environment. Over the last several years the work, in its various forms, has had a number of exhibitions both in this country and abroad, including international venues such as Siggraph and Ars Electronica.

Q: In what way did the UCLA design and computer science team contribute to *The Bush Soul* project?

RA: The design students were basically involved with developing the visual form of the piece, including the characters and the different features of the landscape environment. The computer science students performed a number of different tasks. For example, one AI (artificial intelligence) student got involved with programming the artificial life component of the piece while a small group of three other students helped build the engine, which is the driving force that renders the 3D. The engine, which was equivalent to, and in some ways better than commercial video game engines, was attached to the behavior scripting language that we had also developed. The intent was to build a virtual reality system that

was easy to use and that would allow a participant to interact with the artificial life forms and their personalities and behaviors. It was a dream come true and something I had wanted to do since the 1980s. Artificial life started to appear at that time, in particular Karl Sims' pioneering work in the field (see chapter 3), but the output required a relatively slow frame-by-frame animation process. It wasn't really until the mid-1990s that you could generate animated A-life forms in real-time.

Q: Can you say what motivated or inspired you to produce *The Bush Soul*?

RA: Well, for one thing I wanted to depart from what was generally happening with virtual reality and avatars, and somehow include the viewer's physical participation and movement in the computer experience. It's a direction that's always been present in my work and I intentionally try to maintain this link. I believe the human body is very important to who we are and where we're going. After being immersed in the computer field for many years I've seen a growing tendency for people to become less connected to their bodies and physical senses. It's the *Neuromancer*[5] idea of transmitting information and images by jacking directly into the brain and bypassing the body. I know that's one way we're headed, but I also feel that there are other avenues that should be explored. So after seeing some of the work that was going on with virtual reality and avatars I decided to look into the possibility of developing an alternative type of interactive VR strategy.

The problem that I found with the design of most avatars is that no real

Facing pages: Installation views of *The Bush Soul* (1997–2000), an interactive virtual environment by Rebecca Allen. Presented as a three-screen panoramic display, this work explores the role of human presence in a world of artificial life.

physical connection exists between the graphic representation of the user – the avatar – and the person operating the system. The intent of most works that used avatars was deliberately to have the user leave his or her physical body, enter the virtual world and, in effect, become the avatar. As I began to consider this issue I came across some rather interesting research material about human consciousness and the soul. I discovered that in West Africa there is a belief that a person has more than one soul and that there is a type of soul called the bush soul that can dwell within a wild animal. In other words, these people accept that they have a soul within their bodies, but they also believe that they have a soul – a separate spirit or life force – that can inhabit a wild animal in the bush. I immediately thought that this would be an appropriate metaphor for the type of avatar I wanted to create within a virtual environment. I could envisage a piece where you could be in a physical place and at the same time you could be in another place – a virtual world – without this sense of losing your body. It would be like having multiple souls.

The Bush Soul, as a concept, was also compatible with my interest in developing A-life forms. One of my aims was to depart from the way virtual space is so often used and to avoid the kind of interactivity so prevalent in today's shoot 'em up video games. I wanted to use a different approach where participants don't become avatars, but rather inhabit highly stylized and independent characters that are, in fact, artificial life forms. As a result, I designed *The Bush Soul* so that when a participant enters the world the characters already have a personality and

are programmed according to certain rules. Essentially, I wanted the participant to travel to a strange and exotic place and to discover and interact with A-life forms that already exist in the environment. The participant's role in *The Bush Soul* isn't to control these characters and to combat a hostile world, but to observe and to communicate with the various inhabitants and to learn how they behave. The more one discovers about the behavior of these artificial life forms, the better one can interact with the virtual environment and experience the potential meaning of the installation.

Q: Would you describe the type of computer interface that allows the user to navigate the installation's virtual environment and participate in the interactive experience?

RA: In the third and final version of *The Bush Soul* we made a very important change in the interface device. In the two earlier versions of the piece we used a standard video game pad to navigate the world, but for *The Bush Soul 3* we developed a haptic force feedback joystick. This device is similar to the type of interface used in car driving games that allows the player to actually feel certain kinds of vibration in the steering wheel when traveling over a bumpy road or experiencing a crash, for example. By using this type of interface in *The Bush Soul*, it was possible for the virtual world to become physically attached to the participant and provide important haptic feedback cues about the activities of the characters and the terrain of the environment.

All images: From *The Bush Soul* (1997–2000), an interactive virtual environment by Rebecca Allen.

7 Telematic art

When English computer scientist Tim Berners-Lee proposed the World Wide Web in 1989, the idea of a graphical interface for a global network seemed like the stuff of science fiction, but within a few short years the web evolved from a fantastic concept to a ubiquitous reality. As telecommunications continues to grow, more and more media artists are attempting to maximize the immense potential of this vast network: the ability to interactively communicate over distance via text, sound and moving images. Although the web was a revolutionary development, it is important to note that the aesthetic possibilities of telematic communications and satellite technology were being investigated and used by artists as far back as the early 1970s. At that time, a small group of forward-looking individuals saw this convergence of telecommunications and computers as an opportunity to develop artistic exchanges of information, sound and images from one part of the world to another in real-time. Their vision was based on a series of still valid strategies such as the exploration of time-space relationships, i.e. the immediacy of electronic transmission, the use of interactivity as a locus for the creative process, and most important of all, the networking of human relationships. The emphasis of their pioneering explorations, like the telematic art forms that were to follow, was on the creative process that takes place between artist and audience, rather than on the work of art itself.

Early excursions into this new field were primitive by today's standards, but had immense technical and artistic implications. For example, as early as 1970, media artist and experimental animator Stan VanDerBeek and his associate Ruth Abraham transmitted a six-by-twenty foot mural from the Massachusetts Institute of Technology to six other locations (including South America) using a Xerox telecopier and a telephone conference hook-up. Several years later, Nam June Paik, Joseph Beuys and Douglas Davis demonstrated the expressive and distributive capability of advanced communications technology by producing a series of telematic performance works for Documenta VI, an international art exhibition in Kassel, Germany. Each artist created their own live television event, which was sent via satellite to more than thirty countries around the world. Their experimental projects were among the first artworks to involve a global distribution of thought without commercial broadcast constraints: in effect, the realization of a free and open telematic alternative to standard communication media.

During this period other artists were beginning to work with rudimentary forms of interactivity, creating dialogical experiences with a simple send/receive approach. In an event organized by the Center for New Arts Activity of New York and by Art Com La Manelle of San Francisco, fifteen hours of interactive transmission between the two cities was accomplished. Also at this time an artwork entitled, *Satellite Ars Project* opened up yet other possibilities, becoming the first linked interactive performance between the east and west coasts of America. Conceived by Kit Galloway and Sherrie Rabinowitz and produced in collaboration with NASA Goddard Space Flight Center in Maryland and the Educational Television Center in Menlo Park, California, the performance consisted of an event shared by two different groups of performers separated by hundreds of miles. Galloway and Rabinowitz went on to create numerous other works, increasingly sophisticated telematic projects that ranged from public participatory pieces to events that combine various disciplines such as poetry, music, dance and the visual arts.

In 1984, the year associated with George Orwell's futuristic novel, video artist, Nam June Paik launched, *Good Morning Mr. Orwell*, a television event that was transmitted via satellite to numerous locations around the world including

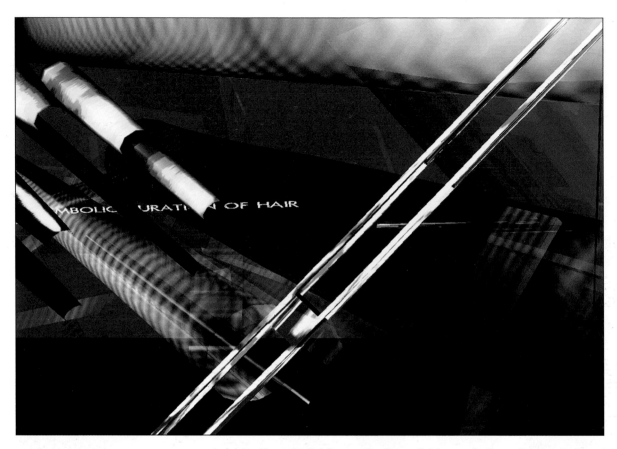

Above: From the 1997 telematic version of *The World Generator/Engine of Desire* produced by Bill Seaman in association with Gideon May.

menu-wheel. A participant can even choose to focus his or her attention solely on the installation's audio capability, generating an environment comprised primarily of sound loops. To control and orchestrate the mobility or kinetic activity of these various components within the virtual world, different types of movement from the "behavior" wheel can be selected. In other words, a specific behavior can be assigned to a 3D object, a text, a still image, a moving picture, or a sound-object. Some of these behavior possibilities include "spin on axis", "spin head over heels", "oscillate up and down", "spiral in and out" and "change scale".

These effects, as well as the installation's other elements, are capable of carrying specific aesthetic content or fields of meaning. As images, texts and sounds are put into play and articulated, ideas and feelings can be explored and developed. The aim of my project, then, is to create a poetic system as well as a functioning discourse mechanism; a meta-machinic assemblage that is designed to actively engage a participant, promote insights into our sense of perception, and elucidate some of the ways we process information and understand the world.

Q: Specifically what kind of ideas and content are contained in the text menu of the installation and how are they employed by the vuser?

BS: *The World Generator* contains an elaborate set of text-objects that I wrote and designed, drawing from many different sources. Essentially, my aim was to write a meta-text that conveys my thoughts about virtual environments. In terms of its operation, a participant can choose lines from the text menu one at a time and place them into the virtual space as visual objects, each with its own location-sensitive audio-text triggering mechanism. As a participant travels through the installation's virtual space and moves close to a 3D text-object, the audio comes up and the participant can hear the line spoken. I used my own voice to produce each spoken line and then entered it into the system. Texture maps and behaviors can also be applied to these text-objects. I wanted to provide the participant with a new sonic-spatial literary form to explore, one that has a versatile and extended range of possibilities.

Q: Would you describe the dialogical component of the online version of *The World Generator* – the ZKM installation – and how it allowed participants located in Germany and other countries to interact with the various structural features of the virtual environment as well as with each other?

BS: Unlike other installations of *The World Generator*, the networked version collapses distance and time and enables participants in remote locations mutually

heighten the potential for constructing satisfying aesthetic environments. It's an approach that might be referred to as "loading the dice", and it's similar to the notion of "canned chance", a technique that Marcel Duchamp explored in his work, *Three Standard Stoppages* (1913–1914).

For me one of the most exciting "random-functions" is called "random-all". When selected, it builds a virtual world in real-time using all the possible variables within the system. Elements from the menu are located randomly in space and combined in various configurations. This "random-all" selection is a particularly good example of what I refer to as "re-embodied" intelligence, a process that is idiomatic to the computer. It results in a beautiful, complex virtual world that is instantly and unpredictably constructed. Once this initial construction stage of "random-all" is completed, the participant can then freely navigate through this virtual world and alter its various features. For example, by using the control panel the vuser can create texture maps, an interesting effect that consists of shrink-wrapping still or moving pictures around 3D objects. Music and spoken lines can also be attached to 3D objects by choosing a sound loop from the appropriate to experience a jointly constructed environment. To establish communication, videophones were used to make a direct connection between these participants. The image that was transmitted by videophone was mapped onto a rectangular object in the shared virtual space. As a result, participants could see and hear each other as well as see and hear what was taking place in the constructed environment. The mapped rectangular object, which served as a video avatar, enabled participants to address each other in a direct manner. They could talk and work together to build a world, ignore each other and do whatever interested them; or they could just use the system to facilitate a conversation or some type of visual interaction. By using the Internet the virtual space of *The World Generator* became a social environment, adding another dimension to the work and expanding its interactive and artistic possibilities.

Q: *The World Generator* **is a collaborative work that involved, in addition to you, programmer Gideon May and musician Tony Wheeler. Would you describe your relationship with these individuals and how the collaboration was structured?**

BS: In 1993 I approached Gideon with a general concept for the work, a project that I had been developing and writing about since 1991. Gideon's field is computer science and he has worked with several other artists on interactive virtual environments. Our relationship involved a great deal of interaction and discussion and together we shared responsibility for the design and production of the installation.

We started by developing my plan for the installation's interface and from that point the project quickly expanded and began to take shape. In 1994 we submitted an application to the Australian Film Commission and received funding to produce the work. The original proposal had many more elements and processes than were made operative, but some of these features may yet be added in future versions. *The World Generator/The Engine of Desire* is the kind of work that one could spend a lifetime on, adding new functionality and re-authoring software for different types of technological environments.

Regarding the audio component of *The World Generator*, I had a clear idea about the musical sounds that I wanted to use and how they should be structured. Tony Wheeler, a musician, joined the project to assist with producing the sound. I sung some of the sequences that I planned to use and from these short sound passages he improvised a set of musical phrases on saxophone. I later chose the musical sounds that I felt were appropriate, constructed loops, and integrated them into the installation's audio system, along with hundreds of techno-ambient sounds consisting of synthetic rhythms, drones and various tonal effects.

It's now quite common to have teams of people working on highly complex technological works. Sometimes these teams have a director who controls the project and at other times the work involves a more democratic type of collaboration; it depends on the project. New technologies present new possibilities and require various kinds of personnel and working methods. Sometimes it's necessary to collaborate with individuals who are highly skilled with certain aspects of technology in order to extend the potential of the work. At other times, research is undertaken to develop entirely new types of technology and this requires yet other kinds of specialists.

Below: From *The World Generator/Engine of Desire* produced by Bill Seaman in association with Gideon May. Installed at the UCLA Visualization Portal (2000–2001), this off-line version featured enhanced interactive media capabilities and a curved 160-degree panoramic screen.

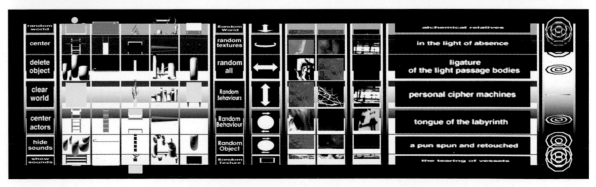

Right and facing page: Two sequential views of *The Hybrid Invention Generator* (2002), an interactive installation produced by Bill Seaman in association Gideon May. In this work viewers are invited to create new "inventions" by selecting existing consumer and industrial products and then hybridizing them into a newly realized object. In one sequence an 18 wheeler and a xylophone are transformed into an *18wheelerxylophone*, and in the other sequence a bike and a conveyor are conjoined to create a bikeconveyor.

On the other hand, I often do much of the media related work for my pieces alone, creating the images, models, video, music, text, and so on. To my mind, one should become active in the processes one enjoys and does well. One should also seek out the resources and personnel needed to develop a work. For example, I'm not a programmer, but I have a very clear idea of the potential of programming and can articulate my interests in a lucid manner to someone else who specializes in programming. My relationship with Gideon May, who is a master programmer, is a case in point.

Q: In your writings and lectures you have used the term "Recombinant Poetics" in reference to your artworks. Would you discuss the meaning of "Recombinant Poetics" and how your installation works are built around this concept?

BS: I'm interested in combinatoric structures that function in the service of emergent meaning. The word, recombinant, which is derived from genetics, is an apt and useful term to describe a certain aspect of my artwork. For example, I think of each of the media elements in *The World Generator* as having a life of its own. The meaning of these elements can shift and mutate as they are combined by the participant, creating ever-changing configurations and juxtapositions. Thus, each time a recombinant poetic work is navigated and actively engaged by a participant, a new potential meaning emerges even though the system is composed of a fixed number of media elements.

Q: What projects have you been working on recently?

BS: We are currently re-authoring *The World Generator/The Engine of Desire* so that it can run on an Apple and/or PC platform. Previously it ran only on SGIs. The interactive spatial text from *The World Generator* was included in the p0es1s show in the Berlin Kulturforum. The work, entitled *T-wo.gen*, was presented in 2004. The digital text files were printed out in multiple font sizes and distributed over four floors of a large atrium as "stick on" poetic sentences. The walls, in effect, became page-like and readable, with sentences ranging in height from two to six inches appearing throughout the exhibition space. A spoken version of the work's text was played over a sound system as part of the piece. Viewers "animated" the text, in this instance, by physically moving through the space of the atrium.

Another recent project that I developed in collaboration with Gideon May is an installation entitled *The Hybrid Invention Generator*. It premiered at the Museum of New Zealand, Te Papa Tongarewa, Wellington in 2002. Like *The World Generator*, it explores computer-based meaning through the inter-author-

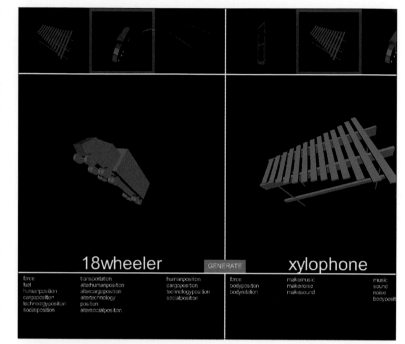

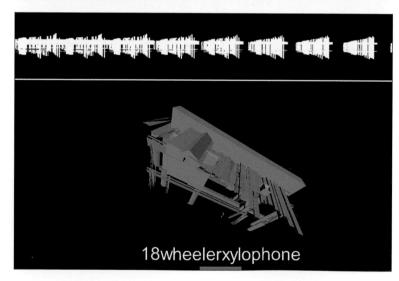

ship and experiential examination of a diverse set of media elements and processes. However, in terms of its programming and actual operation a very different kind of generative process was employed by viewers, one that focused on the virtual construction of hybrid "inventions". For example, by using the system's interactive menu and database, a viewer could combine any two 3D graphic images of existing consumer and industrial products, and then creatively

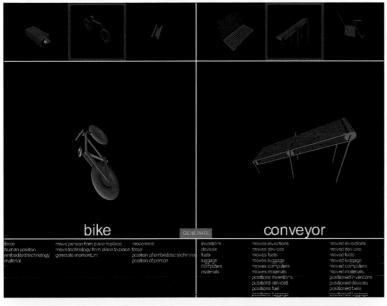

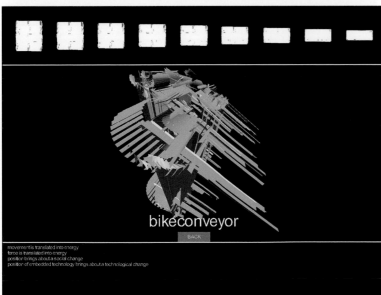

These different sets of media elements can be combined to convey fields of meaning through direct interaction with the system. As individuals engage the work they become dynamically involved in the construction of hybrid inventions as well as in the construction of emergent meaning. The results of this open-ended process can present off-kilter and surreal-like juxtapositions, providing a techno-poetic environment that is capable of engendering rich associative and contemplative experiences.

Q: How was the piece physically configured and what kind of interface was used?

BS: *The Hybrid Invention Generator* functioned via a touch screen interface and projection system. The touch screen was used to access the program and to create imagery that concurrently appeared on the projection screen. Two scrolling sets of various kinds of objects were presented on the touch screen monitor in the form of still 3D computer models. A visitor to the installation could move this "conveyor belt" of objects and observe various kinds of abstract "inventions" – everyday objects such as a bicycle, a Ferris wheel, a cargo plane and so forth. Each 3D object that's provided via the scrolling menu has a specifically authored database, supplying additional information related to a set of potential ways of understanding these objects in terms of "Input", "Functionality" and "Output". The user of the system can select a particular object from the menu simply by touching the screen. A single object is then presented on half of the screen. This object, which appears as a 3D model, can be moved and oriented in space by the participant. The user can then select a second object from the alternative scrolling menu. Once the second object is chosen, a juxtaposition of the two objects is presented – one on the left side of the monitor and the second on the right side. A different audio track accompanies each object and becomes part of the process. When the participant touches "Generate", a hybrid invention is created.

In respect to the work's computer program, an elaborate set of "conjunction codes" was developed that are capable of describing the functional connection between the two chosen objects. These descriptions lend an operative logic to the system, transcending a merely formal/aesthetic intermingling of the objects. The new hybrid inventions that are generated and which appear on the large projection screen can vary widely in terms of their visual appearance and potential functionality. Sometimes they can be highly suggestive of a workable mechanical device, while at other times they can be contemplative in nature, or even humorous. By facilitating the translation and output of imagery, the "conjunction codes" provide a malleable field of possibilities and offers each participant a different experience.

hybridize them into a newly realized object. An airplane and a bike could be digitally combined to create an amalgamated form of *airplanebike*, or an 18-wheeler and a xylophone could be conjoined to generate a 3D model of an *18wheelerxylophone*. The work, which is essentially designed to explore the possibilities of "machinic genetics", is not only concerned with the visualization of hybrid objects, but also with the generative possibilities of related digital audio.

Q: What are you planning to do next?

BS: I'm currently working on a major project that's entitled *The Thoughtbody Environment*. It essentially involves generating a model for an electrochemical computer. Physicist and theoretical chemist Otto Rössler is collaborating with me on the project. He's invited me to be a visitor at his "Artificial Human Intelligence" lab at the University of Tübingen (Germany) and to participate in the development of the model. We've been carrying on conversations relating to endophysics since we first met in Budapest in 1999 and when we met more recently at a conference in Zurich, Switzerland in 2003 we began discussions related to the practical requirements for creating an electrochemical computer. The idea is to study the functionality, physics and biomechanics of the body at the deepest levels and to use this research to build a model of these processes. This model, in effect, would be a starting point for the creation of a self-aware biomachine: an electrochemical computer. As part of the project we are also planning to make a series of virtual environments in order to visualize these processes. These virtual environments would become part of a series of installations that have both digital and analog elements. I exhibited an initial work that was inspired by these conversations at the 2005 Cyberfest in Cambridge, Massachusetts. The piece, which was entitled *The Thoughtbody Environment* was comprised of projected video imagery, poetic and didactic texts, audio, and a series of large still photo blow-ups, fifty-eight by forty-seven and a half inches in size. A major component of our proposed project will be a dynamic association-based database housing poetic works, didactic texts, multiple formats of media files and Internet links to external URLs. Computer scientist David Durand will function as the programmer/collaborator for this phase of the project, the first iteration of which will premiere in 2006/2007. I have also been discussing aspects of the project with the scientists Peter Cariani (Tufts University) and Walter Ratjen (University of Tübingen).

Q: Do you believe there is a hierarchy of media in the arts today? For example do you think that the computer and other advanced technologies have a greater potential for creating works of art than so-called traditional forms of expression.

BS: I'm interested in computer-based interactive environments that enable the intermingling of many different kinds of media elements and processes. In this sense, I'm not interested in hierarchical relationships, but rather I try to enable those who participate in the work to make personal choices about which media elements are to be explored during the interactive experience. Each media element carries a particular meaning-force and each participant carries a personal history that also brings meaning to the work. It's a dynamic process, an ongoing combinatoric activity that facilitates emergent meaning and contributes to the evocation of a work's environment.

In general, I think that computer-based works such as virtual environments and other types of interactive art forms are just beginning to be explored. The ability to call up media elements from various sources and interact with them in a dynamic fashion opens up a great many possibilities for the production and distributions of new artworks. For example, networked art pieces that are capable of accessing audiovisual materials from disparate international localities, as well as bringing together distant participants, present an exciting set of creative possibilities. However, notwithstanding the exciting potential of these new developments, I believe that each medium, whether it involves technology or hand-generated processes, has its own special characteristics and artistic qualities.

Q: What kinds of changes do you see ahead for media in the next five to ten years? Do you think these changes that are in the offing will have a significant effect on the art market or on the art world at large?

BS: In terms of major changes in media, I believe nanotechnology – biomechanics at the molecular level – will bring about a complete paradigm shift. As it emerges and becomes generally operational, many new media technologies will be born and existing ones will go through dramatic changes. It will undoubtedly have a significant impact on the way we practice and perceive art.

In regard to the so-called art market, historically there has been a tendency to favor collectible, saleable items. I'm happy to have my work collected, but generally speaking, there needs to be a dramatic change in the attitude of museum curators, private collectors and critics if media art is going to become part of the mainstream. Based on my own experiences and observations over the last couple of decades, the production and exhibition of digital art has largely been a separate universe that runs parallel to the traditional museum and gallery system. However, I think that change is possible; perhaps it's even inevitable that new technological art forms will become more generally accepted in the future.✧

From a written interview, 2002 and 2005.

Jane Prophet

British media artist Jane Prophet has produced an extraordinary body of multi-media works, highly imaginative synthetic worlds derived from the fusion of art, digital systems and the fundamental processes of nature. A major focus of her creative output concerns the ways in which new digital technologies are changing the triadic relationship of audience, artists and artifact. Using an interdisciplinary approach to form and content Prophet builds on a background in video, performance and real-time graphics while reaching out to advanced methods of digital visualization that involve interactivity, telecommunications and artificial life.

One of Prophet's best-known hyperanimated works is a web-based project entitled *TechnoSphere* (1995–2002).[6] Produced in collaboration with Gordon Selley, Mark Hurry and a team of associates, *TechnoSphere* is comprised of a 3D computer-generated world inhabited by futuristic-looking artificial life forms. These life forms – digital creatures that have their own characteristics and behaviors – are assembled by users from archetypal parts provided by the website. Once these constructed forms are activated, users can track their subsequent "lives" as they evolve and function over time in their simulated environment. *TechnoSphere* allows multiple users to participate freely in a complex online experience, an enchanting surrealistic adventure that challenges the imagination and provides important insights into the ecological aspects of existence. Since its inception *TechnoSphere* has been awarded numerous honors for its distinctive artistic contribution and has been internationally recognized as one of the first examples of an online A-life ecosystem.

Above: Landscape scenes from *TechnoSphere* (1995–2002), a telematic work produced by Jane Prophet and associates. Conceived as a 3D digital world, *Technosphere* is inhabited by artificial life forms built and controlled by World Wide Web Users. Tens of thousands of creatures are "live" in the world at any one time, all competing to survive. They eat, fight, mate and create offspring that evolve and adapt to their environment.

Above: From *TechnoSphere* (1995–2002), produced by Jane Prophet and Associates. Ground level views of *TechnoSphere*'s crowded plains showing some of the 77,000 animated A-life creatures.

Born in 1964, Prophet graduated in fine arts from Sheffield Hallam University in 1987 and received an MA degree in Electronic Graphics from Coventry University in 1989. She later earned a PhD at Warwick University, further pursuing her interest in digital technology and the artistic use of computer imaging. Web pieces by Prophet, in addition to *TechnoSphere*, include *The Heart of the Cyborg* (1995) and *Swarm* (1996). Numbered among her other achievements are *Conductor* (2000), *The Landscape Room* (2001) and *Decoy* (2001). Prophet has exhibited widely at numerous festivals, galleries and art centers including Ars Electronica, Linz, Austria, Institute of Contemporary Art, London, Kiasma Museum of Contemporary Art, Helsinki, the 48th Melbourne International Film Festival, Australia, and Beall Center for Art and Technology, University of California, Irvine. She has also written extensively on the use of computer technology in art and design, presenting papers at conferences and lecture series throughout the UK

and Europe as well as New Zealand, the USA and Canada. Currently affiliated with the University of Westminster, she is Professor of Visual Arts and New Media, and Joint Director of the Center for Arts Research, Technology and Education.

Interview with JANE PROPHET

Q: Your early work as a student primarily involved performance art and video. At what point did you make the transition to digital media and telecommunications?

Jane Prophet: While I was completing my undergraduate studies at Sheffield Hallam University I was awarded a three-year studentship by the British Academy to do post graduate work. I asked visiting artists what they would do with the studentship if they were in my position and they all suggested that I learn something new and apply my ideas to the latest developments in media. So I decided to pursue a BA in Electronic Graphics at Coventry University. I was a bit put off by the term 'graphics' in the course title, but I was assured that I could continue my work in the fine arts. Electronic graphics and computer technology were extremely limited in 1989 and I found my first attempts at 3D modeling by typing in X,Y,Z co-ordinates very tedious and frustrating. But I carried on mainly because I discovered hypertext software and was excited about its potential for creating non-linear networked databases. It was amazing then to realize that there was a corresponding relationship between hypertext and the way I conceptualized when I was sketching ideas for performances and installations ... It all seems very obvious to me now, but at the time I was not familiar with the issues of non-linearity, interaction and the myriad questions these digital strategies raise about narrative and meaning.

In terms of actually making images, Macintosh and PC systems did nothing to help me realize my ideas as a visual artist. As technologies I found them interesting, but as graphic tools I simply couldn't relate to them. I went back to using text and made numerous small-scale animations, both 2D and 3D works, most of which were naive, dull and generally unsuccessful. Yet I remained excited by the concepts behind these experiments even though I was unable to bring them to full realization. Later, when I went to Warwick University to do a PhD in traditional text based theory, I began to understand better the power and potential of digital technology and how I might use it more affectively to express my ideas. *TechnoSphere*,[7] which I made in collaboration with Gordon Selley and others while at Warwick, was the first really cohesive computer-based work that I produced.

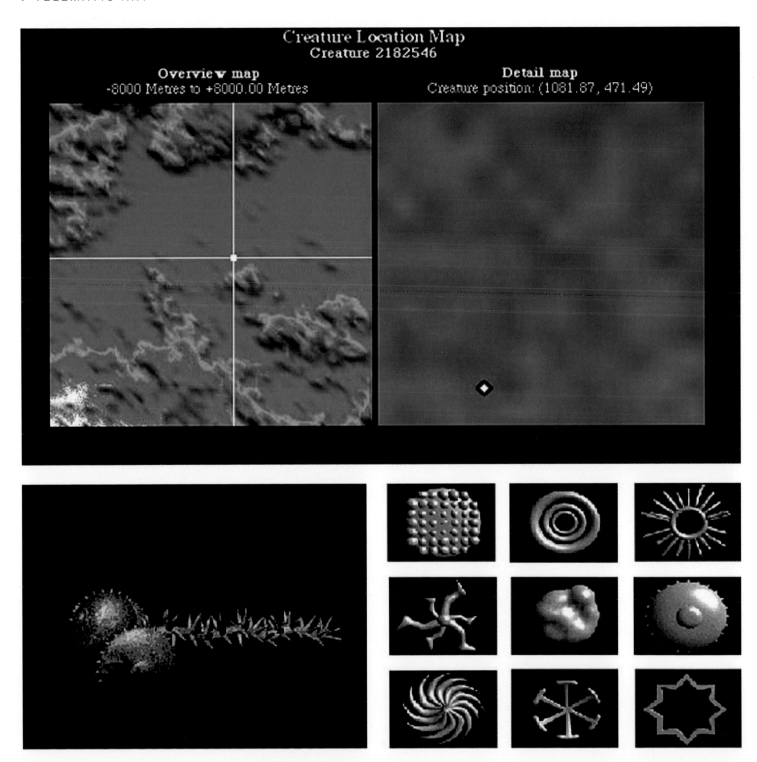

Left: From *TechnoSphere* (1995–2002). produced by Jane Prophet and associates. By typing in an ID number users can view a 2D map of the digital environment that shows the location of their creatures. In this instance the small white marker on the right indicates that the creature is "dead".

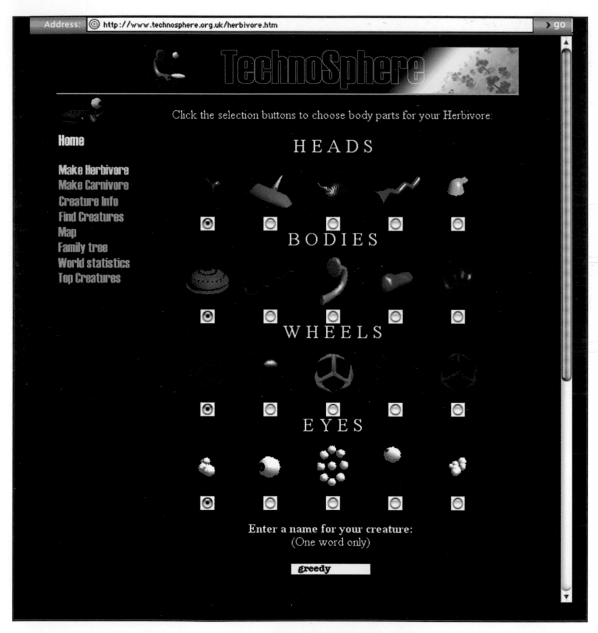

Gordon and I met in 1989 at Coventry University. He was doing his PhD and was sponsored by Rediffusion Flight Simulation, a company that was interested in his research. Originally a graphic artist, Gordon's PhD was concerned with making realistic simulations of trees and fog using fractals.[8] He and I used to have long discussions about various ways to interpret aesthetically the landscape and graphically simulate nature. *TechnoSphere* grew out of those talks

and out of my interest in using digital technologies to make works that involved viewer interaction, a relatively new artistic direction at the time – especially in the UK.

Q: *TechnoSphere* has gone through several changes or iterations. Precisely, how many versions of this piece have been created and what was the chronology of this process?

JP: *TechnoSphere* started in 1994 as an idea that everyone said wouldn't work. Essentially our concept involved creating an A-life website. In 1994 the web was relatively undeveloped in terms of its visual capability, a predominantly grey place with black text and the occasional image aligned left. And the introduction of background gifs, which were perceived by many artists and designers as a major development for the most part only spawned horribly designed web sites with 'busy' backgrounds that made reading impossible. So initially, *TechnoSphere* was not designed primarily as a visual experience, although we did try to push the graphics as far as a slow modem and simple HTML would let us. It was primarily an idea that developed out of our mutual thinking about nature and the artistic possibilities of interaction and text.

In all, there have been three versions of *TechnoSphere*. *TechnoSphere 1* was produced with the assistance of Tony Taylor Moran, with the A-life engine developed by Gordon Selley along with Julian Saunderson and Rycharde Hawkes. One of the defining characteristics of making online artworks is the fact that there is no real sense of 'closure'. Users understand this and expect interactive sites to change and develop over time. Since its inception *TechnoSphere* has been a 'process-based' artwork and has been continuously evolving. Versions *1* and *2* of *Technosphere* define major developmental stages in the project. Changes in between versions *1* and *2* consisted of gradual alterations; typical of the iterative way long-term projects evolve. In the 2003 online version, *TechnoSphere 2*, Gordon has completely rewritten the A-life engine based on his experience with the software since 1995. The website is more interactive now and has been designed to facilitate further upgrades as well as an increase in interactivity by users.

TechnoSphere 3 is the real-time 3D graphic version that we developed for the National Museum of Photography Film and TV in Bradford, UK. We had been exploring the possibilities of real-time 3D design for a while and when we were presented with an opportunity to have the piece permanently installed at the Museum, it gave us the incentive to complete the project. The actual production work was done in collaboration with Mark Hurry and his company Digital Workshop Ltd. This latest version currently does not have a link to the web, but it will have one in the future. It will also be designed so that duplicates of the software can be installed at multiple sites.

Q: Would you describe the form and content of the on-line version of *TechnoSphere* and generally what a visitor to the website experiences?

JP: *TechnoSphere* is an attempt to create an on-line virtual environment that enables many users to interact with numerous artificial life forms. Through this interaction users simultaneously affect a digital ecology and engage in simple dramatic narratives built around the artificial creature's day-to-day behavior in a virtual world. By participating, users become part of the larger online community that surrounds *TechnoSphere* and that influences the development of the artificial life program itself.

The *TechnoSphere* concept is unique in that it combines artificial life, the Internet and in its latest version, real-time 3D graphics. It has already attracted over 650,000 users who have created over a million creatures. The digital ecology of *TechnoSphere*'s 3D world depends on the participation of an online public who access the world via the Internet. Users create their own artificial life forms, building carnivores or herbivores from component parts, including heads, bodies, eyes and wheels. Their digital DNA or genetic specification is linked to each component part of these A-life forms and determines rates of motion, visual perception, rates of digestion and so forth. Once an A-life creature is built, users name their digital creature, tag it with their email address and launch it into the 3D world. As the creatures grow, give birth, move, evolve and die, they send brief email messages back to the users that designed them. These messages – in effect "postcards" home – provide users with key events in the artificial lives of the creatures. Users can visit the website and see 2D snapshots of their beast at any time. They can check family trees, statistics about the 3D world, and trace the activity of other creatures and the users that designed them. For example, if users are interested in finding out more about a creature that their beast has interacted with they can use the ID number of the other creature, which can be obtained via email.

The *TechnoSphere* homepages, which are made by users as an outgrowth of their involvement, contribute to the creation of a networked society; they act as an interface between the human world and the A-life system that is *TechnoSphere*. The map function on the website, which is continuously updated, tracks creatures in real-time with an 'X' marks-the-spot. As users reload the map page they are able to see various activities taking place such as carnivores approaching their creature or their creature merging with another creature during predation or

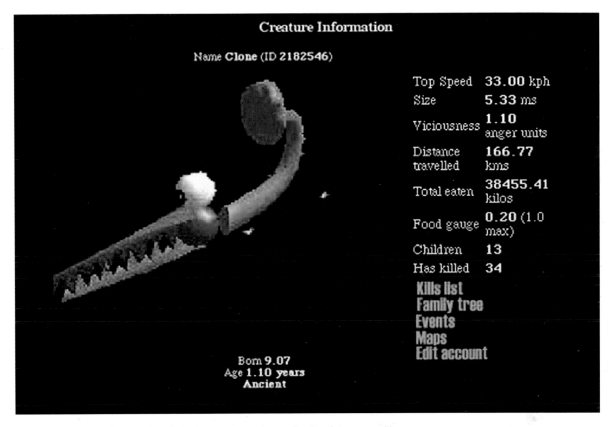

mating. This is graphically simplistic, but users tend to make the data compelling by 'filling in the gaps' of the narrative and by personalizing events. For example, while watching the map function page, one user wrote:

> "… My new creature, a carnivore, is called *Amazing Salamander Twist*. Its number is 77366 and you can monitor *Twist* at the above address. The picture makes it look as though its eye is stuck on its teeth. Now there's an evolutionary advantage …".

The creative process that drives *TechnoSphere* goes beyond Gordon Selley, Mark Hurry or myself and involves all the visitors that make creatures and participate in the website. For example, the constant injection of new creatures made by users interrupts the ecosystem, generating new possibilities and altering the environment. Some users make just one creature while others return time and time again, making new beasts as they 'interpret' their creature's life, compare it to the "Top Creatures" list featured on the website, and try to make a faster, hungrier or more fecund artificial life forms.

TechnoSphere supports many tens of thousands of competing life forms; typically 20,000 creatures are alive at any one time. The website is scaleable and

Above: From *TechnoSphere* (1995–2002), produced by Jane Prophet and associates. One of the digital creatures listed on the "Top Creatures" page of the *TechnoSphere* website.

Facing page: From *TechnoSphere* (1995–2002), produced by Jane Prophet and associates. Users create their own artificial life forms, building carnivores and herbivores from component parts (heads, bodies, eyes and wheels). Once a life form is built, users name their digital creature and place it in the 3D virtual world of *TechnoSphere*.

Above: A remote installation view of *Web of Life* (2002), a networked multi-user work produced by Jeffrey Shaw and ZKM Associates.

of stylized imagery. Rapidly improving silicon-based techniques will contribute to these advancements in digital imaging: however, silicon as a matrix of information technology is expected to reach its fundamental limits in the next decade or so. Researchers are now in the process of developing a variety of new and exotic replacements including a promising technology known as quantum computing,[1] which stores data in nuclear spins of individual atoms and molecules. The non-intuitive laws of quantum mechanics potentially allow for a huge leap in computational power, a development that could have a significant impact on future methods of visualization. However, while laboratory tests have demonstrated the feasibility of this technology, a practical quantum computer has yet to be built.

There are also indications that real-time as well as stored media information will be presented to viewers on high resolution multi-format screens that vary in size from cell phones and other kinds of small portable devices, to multi-monitor displays and large-scale projection screens. Dance, opera and the theatrical proscenium could also be transformed in the not too distant future by innovative digital imaging applications. Animator Diana Walczak (chapter 5) believes that virtual stage sets and environments – large-scale projections of 3D computer animation used in conjunction with live performance – have the potential to create a new and expanded kind of theatrical experience. Her views and her actual work

in the field of digital theatre raise important questions about the formal possibilities of performance and challenge conventional notions of theatrical time and space.

Another promising technological development involves wearable computer systems. These systems, which are actually attached to the body and allied with the senses in one way or another are already beginning to be used by scientists, engineers and a number of media artists. One example of this new trend involves special eyeglasses that display information and graphics while at the same time allowing the wearer to see and interact with people and objects. Because a person using these spectacles is not required to sit in front of a monitor, it is possible to access data while moving freely throughout the physical environment. Always turned on and in contact with the wearer, this type of viewing system provides a form of augmented reality that could change our relationship to computers and open up new avenues for artistic expression. On the other hand, there are forms of virtual reality being developed that may eliminate the use of special glasses or a head-mounted display. Instead, other kinds of viewing technologies – possibly improved lenticular lens-like screens – could provide effective and more accessible 3D stereoscopic environments.

Undoubtedly the Internet will be an immensely important computer graphics system during the next decade and its interactive capability is certain to be enhanced with a variety of newly designed interfaces. As the world of web design progresses the development and use of animated avatars (virtual on-line characters) could play a major role, providing intelligent agents that viewers can interact with as they do with people. Having such avatars could radically change the way artists access the web and carry on dialogues with other individuals, especially those located in foreign countries. For example, large amounts of information – languages, social customs and other practical data – could be stored in these avatars to help overcome cultural barriers and create global artistic experiences. Although this notion of art and communications may seem remote, there are even more extreme and sublime applications being contemplated. For instance, media artist Rebecca Allen (chapter 8) envisages a time in the future when people will spend much of their lives in data space interacting with each other in 3D virtual worlds. She suggests that these worlds – computer-generated environments depicting many aspects of life – could possibly include highly sophisticated avatars: graphic representations of us that will embody our souls and consciousness. Avatars of the future, Allen speculates, will become our body, another container for our spirit.

Within the next few years it is quite likely that there will be a plethora of miniature audiovisual devices, with and without wires, permeating the physical environment. These devices will not be thought of as computers but as an integral part of architecture, appliances, cars, toys and even clothing. Paralleling these projected lines will be the continued growth of both wireless broadband transmission and fiber optics, further enabling the widespread distribution of high-resolution media. The implementation of interactive television,[2] the advent of digital cinema,[3] and the eventual use of satellite transmission by motion picture theaters fitted out with large-scale computer display equipment are also on the horizon. The transition to many of these computer-mediated imaging and communications technologies, although not easy, is likely to take place in the short term, while it may take decades before others become feasible.

Future developments will depend on overcoming an array of complicated and intertwined factors: social, economic and cultural. However, such problems are typical of emerging technological media. In just the last thirty years many forms of visualization – film, analog computer imaging and even methods of digital animation – either no longer exist or have undergone considerable transformation; it is the nature of technological progress that changes occur at a rapid pace and models soon become outdated. Nevertheless, the question that concerns many artists is not about the volatility of new processes and equipment, but whether in terms of expense and complexity, creative individuals will have easy access to these expressive capabilities. The answer to that question seems to be yes. However, although there is reason to be optimistic, there is also reason to be concerned. Most speculation and planning, for example, tends to focus on industry hardware, software and distribution issues, with insufficient regard for the role of the independent artist. All the same, the quality and promise of digital media largely depends on freethinking individuals with powerful imaginations who are willing to forge new directions. The works of independent artists are important not only because they provide stimulating concepts and techniques, but also because they provide alternative directions that counter (but frequently complement) the huge technological and ideological apparatus of mass media and the troubling effects of large-scale cultural conditioning.

As the motion picture industry (film, television, computer gaming, etc.) becomes subject to the economic pressure of widespread global distribution, correspondingly there has been an enormous increase in production costs. Although, these production costs also encourage investment in the development of new digital technologies they have, from a creative standpoint, exacted a substantial price: a high degree of standardization. With its tendency to optimize existing formulas for success, the motion picture industry has at the same time severely inhibited the progress of technological and artistic experimentation. Still, the new availability of relatively low cost digital equipment and the accessibility of computerized networks have provided, and will undoubtedly continue to provide

Left: Still from a 3D animated projection by Robert Darroll. This projection was used as a virtual theatrical set for Kiyoshi Furukawa's interactive opera, *To the Unborn Gods* (1997).

in the future, an effective platform for the evolution of independent, experimental and personal works of art. Hyperanimation is a case in point. A new breed of artists, some of whom are represented in these pages, have developed technological working methods that challenge the homogeneity of the motion picture industry, create fresh artistic content and suggest future alternatives to conventional commercial formats and narrative dramaturgy. The influence of their innovative works, like the various experimental film and video movements of the twentieth century, will be felt beyond the art world as fresh modes of imaging, communications and cinematic space are developed and realized.

The convergence of aesthetics and biotechnology

While in certain ways digital expression maintains a connection to established artistic traditions, in other ways it represents a radical break. As computer tools are integrated into the creative process a new type of thinking is required that involves explicit rules and abstract structures, thus stimulating a change in the very nature of expressive language. Moreover, digital imaging has mediated a potent interdisciplinary approach, leading to the exploration (and anticipation) of entirely new and intriguing art forms that could not have been conceived otherwise. For instance, a growing number of media artists are drawing inspiration from the sciences, in particular the promise of biologically based disciplines such as artificial life, genetic engineering and nanotechnology. These creative individuals are interested in the artistic potential of natural processes (vegetal growth patterns, molecular behavior, living systems) and the use of a softer, wetter and more

Above: A detail of *Nature is Leaving Us* (1989), a multimedia theatrical production by Miroslaw Rogala. [Photo documentation courtesy of Rogala Studio/Outerpretation, Chicago, Illinois.]

These new interdisciplinary developments have substantially broadened the creative possibilities of "computer art" and redefined the term's original meaning. It no longer simply refers to a process in which the computer is used only as a tool with the artist making all the choices. This commonly held notion has been extended, indeed transfigured by an approach in which the computer is programmed to simulate the laws of evolution. With this process, mutating images are generated, producing endless combinations of shapes, colors and textures while the artist assumes the role of metacreator. It is a form of art making that is idiomatic to the computer and syntactically contoured by the creative act of writing code. In order to fully appreciate works produced with the principles of artificial life, it is important to recognize that although the imagery is self-propagating, it originates with the artist and his or her ability to imaginatively design and manipulate algorithms. As the use of artificial life and genetic algorithms continue to develop, and as aesthetics and biotechnology converge and expand, exciting new directions are being contemplated that will likely require a change in attitude about the way art can be produced and experienced. Artist and computer programmer Jon McCormack (chapter 3), a pioneer in the field of organic animation, asserts that entirely new kinds of artistic expression – worlds never before imagined – are possible through the digital implementation of biological principles. He points out that a major tenet of artificial life holds that humans and the so-called natural environment are only one instance of life – "life as we know it" – and that there are more general mechanisms that define life – "life as it could be". According to McCormack it is an idea that applies to synthesis in general and has immense implications for the future production of art works. He concludes that artistic creativity should not be constrained by our perception of "reality" because "reality" is only a subset from a far greater set of possibilities.

organic technology that betokens a clear split from the mechanistic paradigm of the industrial age.[4]

An area of new scientific investigation that has already yielded impressive artistic results – and has significant future possibilities – is artificial life, a field that attempts to study and understand biological life by digitally synthesizing artificial life forms. The discipline is very broad, ranging from artificial ecosystems and molecular evolution to interactive environments and artificial morphogenesis. One type of artificial life that is of special interest to artists involves the use of genetic algorithms. It is an approach that is being used to produce various types of synthetic imagery – both still pictures and animated works. Artists are discovering that by programming with genetic algorithms surprisingly complex and beautiful pictorial forms can actually be digitally bred and mutated in ways that simulate the organic processes found in nature. It is a method of creative production that is characterized by a unique and compelling feature: the ability to separate the image from a unilaterally controlled context and create unpredictable visual structures. Thus, unlike the fixed linear form of conventional motion pictures, for example, it is possible to digitally produce a universe of free variables that exist in event-worlds that are continuously evolving and interacting with one and another. The imagery that results from the use of genetic algorithms is not static or sequentially predetermined, but rather is a self-generated event, an organic creation that is initiated by the artist. This form of expression constitutes a clear departure from mainstream art and cinema; it radically challenges our conventional concepts of pictorial representation and brings into question the traditional role of the artist.

Whereas important hyperanimated works have already been produced with artificial life principles, generally the artistic application of biotechnology in its various forms is just beginning to be explored; much of it is still in a conceptual stage. On the horizon, for example, is a field of research – microelectro mechanical systems or MEMS – that could trigger new methods of visualization. MEMS, millimeter-scale machines etched from silicon, are used in the field of nanotechnology. These lilliputian devices are opening up whole new frontiers in a wide variety of areas from communication and energy production to bioengineering. Conceived as implants, MEMS could be used to facilitate the artistic process at the molecular level, providing a basis for engaging the human sensory system in entirely new ways. Although this prospect is speculative and difficult to imagine, some researchers believe that micro machines may have even wider applications. They theorize that MEMS could be implanted, not only into our biological systems

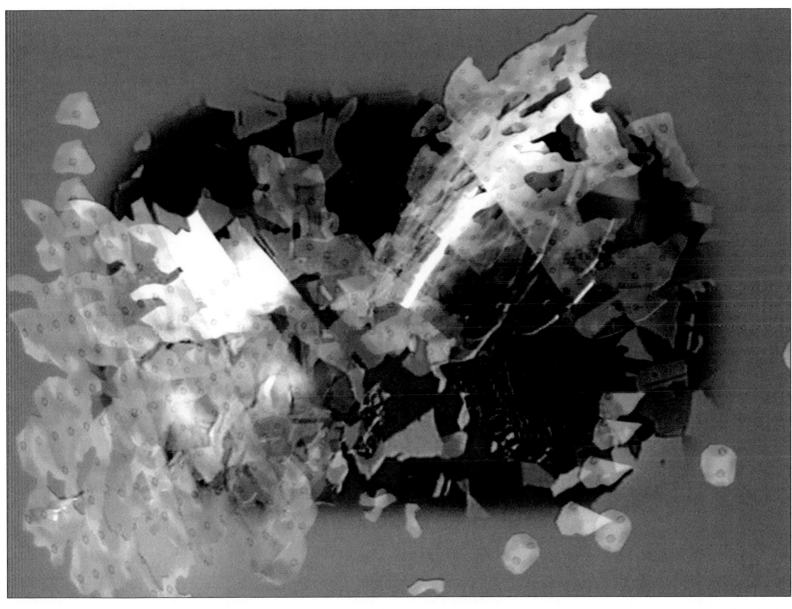

and brains, but also into our physical surroundings. The walls and objects of architectural interiors, for example, could be imbued with characteristics of the virtual world, thus creating environments that are subject to change in terms of their function and visual appearance. As promising as MEMS may appear, it should be noted that their use in the field of nanotechnology is still in an early phase of development and has yet to be used in the production of actual artworks. Nonetheless, multimedia specialist Bill Seaman (chapter 7) predicts that once nanotechnology and its various applications become fully operational it will bring about a paradigm shift in the art world; new forms of media will be developed and existing ones will undergo major changes. Seaman believes that nanotechnology will revolutionize our concepts of expression, extend our methods of communication and have a significant effect on the way we practice and perceive art.

Another possible direction that could alter methods of digital visualization involves the future effects of biotechnology on software development. For instance,

some computer researchers speculate that in order for large systems to move forward in terms of processing power a different programming style will be required, one in which software is a "living" entity, organically grown rather than coded. This concept also fits with other forecasts that large systems, in the minds of users, will be conceived as ecologies rather than machines. Along these lines artist and futurist Roy Ascott (chapter 7) predicts that "moistmedia" – post biological systems – will lead to a deceleration and replacement of the digital determinism that has marked the beginning of the twenty-first century. In 1997, while living with the Kuikuru Indians of Brazil, Ascott observed that their tribal life consisted of a certain fundamental type of syncretism – i.e. the mixture of diverse forms and practices inside a system – and was impressed by its potential for shaping cultural expression, behavior and values. It is within this context that he feels the interaction of art, biological systems and technology will provide fresh models and metaphors and will contribute to reframing our concepts of self and society.

As science and digital processes converge there is increased speculation that the modernist vision of a rational, functional future comprised of industrial-age tools and materials may be superceded by a complex and pervasive form of biotechnology: self-replicating, self-repairing systems modeled after natural processes. These new systems – like human biological systems – would potentially be able to adapt, learn and evolve, re-directing the design of their creations toward the organic. Although the joining of biology and digital visualization has important implications, the future significance of any hybrid art form that may result will

have far less to do with its "technology" and more to do with the aesthetic and ethical contributions that emerge. The great art of the Renaissance, after all, was not about the science of perspective, but rather about a fresh and life-affirming vision of humanity. Conceivably, the next generation of media artists could face a task every bit as lofty and challenging as the tasks that confronted Leonardo and his peers.

Finally, it should be noted that while the relationship of techno-scientific developments and art are extending the possibilities for new forms of creative expression, their relationship has also released a powerful new dynamic that in many ways will be difficult to predict, especially in the long term. Not surprisingly, any speculation about the future of Hyperanimation, including its potential offspring and digital permutations, tends to pose as many questions as it does answers. All the same, many of the artists represented in these chapters believe that computing power will progress far beyond the present standards of artificial intelligence and biotechnology, redefining "thought" and perhaps even what we consider "life". This radical view of the future is difficult to visualize and even more difficult to fathom in terms of art and what it would be like under these extreme circumstances. However, these trajectories are not so much "science fiction", but rather they are based on evolving technological and biological developments and a vast potential that seems far from being fully realized. Whether looked upon with wonderment or consternation, it may take the rest of the twenty-first century before many of these forward-looking ideas can be developed and tested. Meanwhile, the field of Hyperanimation will continue to grow and create

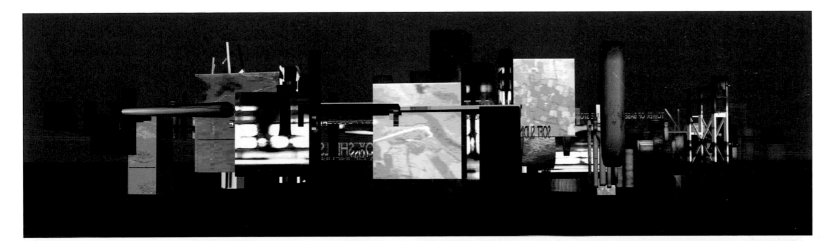

Left: From *The World Generator/Engine of Desire* (2000–2001), an interactive installation produced by Bill Seaman in association with Gideon May.

experiences never before attempted, eloquently reminding us that the effectiveness of science and technology in the service of art is determined by the vitality of human imagination.

Notes

1. Assuming miniaturization of microprocessors continues to follow the rapid pace predicted by Moore's Law (transistors per integrated circuit will double every eighteen months), scientists anticipate that the quantum level will be reached in ten to fifteen years. Thus, quantum computing (computing at the molecular level) is currently being explored as a possible next step. Although still in an early stage of development quantum computing could embody a new paradigm, offering the potential for immense advances in power and speed and suggesting deep fundamental links between quantum theory, computer science and information theory. See Michael A. Nielson and Issac L. Chang, *Quantum Computation and Quantum Information*. Cambridge, UK: Cambridge University Press, 2000.

2. Interactive television (iTV), which at the present time is relatively undeveloped, promises to extend the viewer's use of television by providing opportunities for participation that are similar to the Internet. For example, interactive television could allow viewers to browse information or topics of interest, personalize their viewing choices, play interactive games, participate in distance learning, carry on e-commerce (shopping, banking, etc.), interact with other viewers, and play an increasingly active role in broadcast programs.

3. Digital cinema, which is produced using computer technology, as opposed to chemicals and celluloid film, is currently redefining the very definition of motion pictures. Some of the developing possibilities that fall under the heading of digital cinema involve the use of virtual reality, synthetic actors, interactivity, telematic imaging, as well as expanded forms of narrative entertainment.

4. For more information about the relationship of living systems and organic technology to the creation of artworks, see Mitchell Whitelaw, *Metacreation: Art and Artificial Life*. Cambridge, MA: The MIT Press, 2004.

wearer as having real three-dimensional depth.

High resolution Refers to a monitor, video card or image that displays fine detail and millions of colors.

Hologram An interference pattern, often using photographic media, that is encoded by laser beams and read by means of a low-power laser beam or white light. This interference pattern can reconstruct a three-dimensional image, thus creating a pictorial illusion that has real depth. No special glasses or viewing device is needed to experience the spatial effect of a hologram.

HTML **H**yper **T**ext **M**arkup **L**anguage, the authoring language used to create documents on the World Wide Web.

Image processing The computerized manipulation of an image – commonly the graphic transformation of a still photograph or video.

Internet A global network connecting millions of computers. More than one hundred countries are linked into exchanges of data, text, images and sound.

Key frame In computer animation, the term refers to a user-defined point where a specific animation event takes place – such as the beginning or end of a motion. The computer then interpolates (or "tweens") the events from key frame to key frame. In a digital video file, the key frame contains the entire image; other frames contain only the information that changes from the previous frame.

Memory Programs and files that are loaded from a disk (or any other input device) into random-access memory (RAM) for easy access during all phases of processing.

Microprocessor An integrated circuit built on a single chip containing the entire central processing unit (CPU) of a computer.

Moist media A hybrid technology that is projected to supplant current digital standards and media applications. Artist Roy Ascott (chapter 7) argues that a whole new substrate of our lived experience is being formed from the technologically driven convergence of bits, atoms, neurons and genes & the BIG BANG. He believes that from the artist's point of view this is creating a new media universe. The first stage of this convergence, according to Ascott, can be seen as the digitally dry data of the computer mixes with the wet biology of living systems, producing a kind of "moist media". The second stage – the advent of nanotechnology – will bring yet another dimension to our constructive urge to build new worlds.

Motion capture An animation technique that usually refers to measuring a person's position in physical space, then recording that information in a computer-usable form. The digital information derived from the live subject's movement is used as source data for animating a 3D computer model of a figure or stylized character.

Nanotechnology A body of technology in which products, objects and processes are created through the manipulation of atoms and molecules. "Nano" refers to a billionth of a meter, which is the width of five carbon atoms.

Network Connection between computers and their peripherals that allow every user to access the computer and communicate with others.

Neural implant A brain implant designed to enhance one's sensory ability, memory or intelligence.

Noise A random sequence of data. Because the sequence is random and without meaning, noise carries no information.

On line The opposite of off line, it transfers data from one device to another via a direct link. On line connections require that the linked devices "understand" their data formats and structures and can keep up with the speed of the data transfer.

Operating system A software program that manages and provides a variety of services to application programs, including user interface facilities and the management of input-output and memory devices.

Paradigm A pattern, model, or general approach to solving a problem.

Particle (or particle-generating) system An animation module for generating and controlling the semi-random behavior of numerous tiny objects (particles), to simulate bubbles, flames, sparks, smoke and the like.

Persistence of vision The tendency of the eye and mind to retain an image for a moment after seeing it, allowing steps of action (as in movie frames) to be perceived as continuous movement. Films project 24 individual frames a second and videos project 30 (or more accurately 29.97 fps.).

Pixel An abbreviation for picture element. The smallest element on a computer screen that holds information to represent a picture. Pixels contain data giving brightness and possibly color at particular points in the picture.

Polhemus tracker A hardware device that tracks the physical movements of the user and sends information about position and orientation to the computer for processing. When attached to a hand-held device, a Polhemus tracker can digitally control and alter the visual, spatial and kinetic features of a virtual scene.

Procedural modeling In 3D modeling, software that utilizes formulae that take into account the randomness of natural phenomena.

Program A set of computer instructions that enables a computer to perform a specific task.

Robotics The science and technology of designing and manufacturing robots. Robotics combines artificial intelligence and mechanical engineering.

Software Information and knowledge used to perform useful functions by computers and computerized devices. Includes, computer programs and their data.

Stereoscopy A technique used to create the illusion of real depth in photographs, motion pictures or other types of graphic imagery. The procedure for creating depth perception in the brain (stereopsis) involves providing the eyes of the viewer with two different flat images representing two slightly different perspectives of the same object. These two separate perspectives are similar to the two perspectives of an object that both eyes normally receive in binocular vision. Special glasses are required for viewing most forms of stereoscopy.

Storyboarding Planning a film or animation by breaking a scene down into a sequence of sketches (on a storyboard) that illustrate the key movements and compositions of the entire work.

Synthesizer An analog device that computes signals in real-time. Synthesizers have been used to electronically generate and process music and moving imagery (video).

Technology An evolving process of tool creation to shape and control the environment. Technology goes beyond the mere fashioning and use of tools. It involves a record of tool making and a progression in the sophistication of tools. It requires invention and is itself a continuation of evolution by other means.

Telematic aesthetics The term refers to the use of computer-mediated telecommunications for the purpose of facilitating artistic exchanges of information, sound and images from one part of the world to another in real-time.

Texture mapping The process of assigning attributes – textures, photos, images, etc., – to the surface of a 3D computer generated object.

Three-dimensional (3D) The term refers to objects that have the three dimensions of height, width and depth. Computer-generated 3D objects can be freely manipulated in computer space.

Three-dimensional object Any three-dimensional object created or used in 3D graphics or animation.

Touch screen An input device that allows the user to operate a computer by simply touching the display screen.

Transform Any operation, such as move, scale, or rotate, that affects the position, size, or shape of a computer generated object.

User interface Generally the term refers to a keyboard, mouse, data glove or other type of device that allows the user to communicate with the operating system and with the computer's audiovisual environment.

Videographic animation A form of real-time analog video animation.

Virtual Not actual, but well-imitated. A 3D computer generated object is a virtual object: it does not exist outside of the computer's memory, but the user can manipulate it (within the computer) as if it actually existed.

Virtual reality The use of computer simulation to create an artificial, three-dimensional environment. Through the use of a head-mounted display or a CAVE system, the viewer can immerse himself or herself in this environment, which provides a convincing replacement for the visual and auditory senses.

Web browser A software application used to locate and display web pages.

Wipe In animation, when one scene is cleared (pushed) off the screen by the next scene.

World Wide Web A system of Internet servers that support specially formatted documents. The documents are formatted in a markup language called HTML (Hyper Text Markup Language) that supports links to other documents that include text, graphics, audio and video files. This allows the user to move from one document to another simply by clicking on hot spots.

10 Bibliography

Ascott, Roy. "Art and Education in the Telematic Culture", *Leonardo*, Supplemental Issue 1988, pp. 7–11.

_____. *Telematic Embrace*. Edited and with an essay by Edward A. Shanken. Berkely, CA: University of California Press, 2003.

_____ and Carl Eugene Loeffer (guests editors). Special Issue. "Connectivity: Art and Interactive Communication", *Leonardo* Vol. 24 No 2, 1991.

Battcock, Gregory. *The New Art* (revised). New York: E.P. Dutton, 1973.

Bendazzi, Giannalberto. *Cartoons: One Hundred years of Cinema Animation*. London: John Libbey & Company Ltd. in association with Indiana University Press, 1996.

Benjamin, Walter. *Illuminations*. New York: Schocken Books, 1978.

_____. *On Walter Benjamin: Critical Essays and Recollections*. (ed.) Gary Smith. Cambridge, MA: The MIT Press, 1988.

Bergson, Henri. *Matter and Memory*. (English translation) London: George Allen and Unwin, 1988.

_____. *Reflections, Essays, Aphorisms, Autobiographical Writings*. (ed.) Peter Demetz. New York: Schocken Books, 1986.

Caldwell, John Thornton. *Electronic Media and Technoculture*. New Brunswick, N.J.: Rutgers University Press, 2000.

Calo, Carole Gold. *Viewpoints: Readings in Art History*. Upper Saddle River, N.J.: Prentice Hall, Inc., 2001.

Costanzo, Jim. "REPOhistory's Circulation: The Migration of Public Art to the Internet", *Art Journal* Vol. 59 No. 4, 2000, pp. 32–37.

Curtis, David. *Experimental Cinema, A Fifty-Year Evolution*. New York: Universe Books, 1971.

Damer, Bruce. *Avatars!, Exploring and Building Virtual Worlds on the Internet*. Berkeley, CA: Peachpit Press, 1998.

Davies, Char. "Ephémère, Reframing Consciousness in the Post Biological Era", *Proceedings of the Second International CaiiA Research Conference*. Roy Ascott, (ed.), Newport: University of Wales College, Centre for Advanced Inquiry into the Interactive Arts, 1998.

Davis, Douglas. *Art in the Future*. New York: Prager Publishers, 1974.

_____ and Simmons, Allison (eds.). *The New Television: A Public/Private Art*. Cambridge MA: The MIT Press, 1977.

Dawkins, Richard. *The Blind Watchmaker*. London: Longman, 1986.

Deepwell, Katy (ed.). "Reverie, Osmose and Ephémère: Dr. Carol Gigliotti Interviews Char Davies", *n. paradoxa, international feminist art journal,* Vol. 9, 2000, pp. 64–73.

Deken, Joseph. *Computer Images: State of the Art*. New York: Stewart, Tabori & and Chang, 1983.

Deleuze, Gilles. *Cinema 1: The Movement-Image*. London: The Athlone Press, 1986.

_____. *Cinema 2: The Time-Image*. London: The Athlone Press, 1989.

Dery, Mark. "Soft Machines", *21-C Scanning the Future*, 1996, pp. 18–23.

Ditlea, Steve. "Lending Your Soul To the Big Screen(s)", *Technology Review*, November–December 1998, pp. 26–27.

Drukrey, Timothy (ed.). *Electronic Culture: Technology and Visual Representation*. New York: Aperture, 1996.

Fifield, George. *"ZKM: The Center for Art and Media"*, *ARTBYTE* Vol. 1 No. 5, 1998–99, pp. 26–31.

Furniss, Maureen. *Art in Motion: Animation Aesthetics*. London: John Libbey & Company Ltd. in association with Indiana University Press, 1998.

_____. "Motion Capture An Overview", *Animation Journal*, Spring 2000, pp. 68–82.

Friedhoff, Richard Mark and Benzon, William. *Visualization: The Second Computer Revolution*. New York, W.H. Freeman and Company by arrangement with Harry N. Abrams, Inc., 1991.

Gibson, William. *Neuromancer*. New York: Ace Books, 1984.

Goldberg, RoseLee. *Performance Art From Futurism To the Present*. London: Thames & Hudson, 2001.

Goodman, Cynthia. *Digital Visions: Computers and Art*. New York: Harry N. Abrams, Inc. in association with the Everson Museum of Art (Syracuse, NY), 1987.

Handhardt, John. (ed.). *Video Culture*. New York: Peregrine Smith Books in association with Visual Studies Workshop Press, 1986.

Hansen, Mark B.N. *New Philosophy for New Media*. Cambridge, MA: The MIT Press, 2004.

Holtzman, Steven. *Digital Mosaics: The Aesthetics of Cyberspace*. New York: Touchstone, 1997.

Kahn, Douglas and Whitehead, Gregory (eds.) *Wireless Imagination: Sound, Radio and the Avamt-garde*. Cambridge, MA: The MIT Press, 1994.

Kelly, Kevin. *Out of Control*. Reading, MA: Addison-Wesley, 1994.

Kerlow, Isaac Victor. *The Art of 3-D Computer Animation and Imaging*. New York: Van Nostrand Reinhold, 1996.

Kester, Grant H. "Aesthetics After the End of Art: An Interview with Susan Buck-Morss", *Art Journal* Vol. 56 No. 1 1997, pp. 38–45.

Kirby, Michael. *Happenings*. New York: E.P. Dutton & Co., Inc., 1966.

Krueger, Myron. *Artificial Reality II*. Reading, MA: Addison-Wesley, 1991.

_____. "Videoplace: A Report From the Artificial Reality Laboratory", *Leonardo* Vol. 18 No. 3, 1985, pp. 145–151.

Kurzewell, Ray. *The Age of Spiritual Machines*. New York: Viking, 1999.

Lawder, Standish. *The Cubist Cinema*. New York: New York University Press, 1975.

Leavitt, Ruth (ed.). *Artist and Computer*. New York: Harmony Books, 1977.

Hershman-Leeson, Lynn. *Clicking In*. Seattle, WA: Bay Press, 1996.

Le Grice, Malcolm. *Abstract Film and Beyond*. Cambridge, MA: The MIT Press, 1977.

Lovejoy, Margot. *Postmodern Currents: Art and Artists in the Age of Electronic Media*. Upper Saddle River, NJ: Prentice Hall, 1997.

Lye, Len. *Figures in Motion, Selected Writings*. (ed.) Wystan, Curnow and Roger Horrocks. Auckland, New Zealand: Auckland University Press, 1984.

Manvell, Roger (ed.). *Experiment in Film*. New York: Arno Press, 1970.

Mekas, Jonas. *Movie Journal: The Rise of a New American Cinema 1959–1971*. New York: Collier Books, 1972.

McLuhan, Marshall. *Understanding Media: The Extensions of Man*. Cambridge, MA: The MIT Press, 1994.

Moholy-Nagy, Lazlo. *Vision in Motion*. Chicago: Hillison and Etten, 1965.

Moritz, William. *Optical Poetry*. London: John Libbey & Company Ltd. in association with Indiana University Press, 2004.

_____. "Some Observations on Non-objective and Non-linear Animation". *Storytelling in Animation: The Art of the Animated Image*, (ed.) John Canemaker. Vol. 2, pp. 21–31, 1988. Published by The American Film Institute in Conjunction with the Second Annual Walter Lantz Conference on Animation.

Moser, Mary Anne with MacLeod, Douglas (eds.). *Immersed in Technology: Art and Virtual Environments*. Cambridge, MA: The MIT Press in association with the Banff Centre for the Arts (Banff, Canada), 1996.

Murray, Janet H. *Hamlet on the Holodeck: The Future of Narrative in Cyberspace*. New York: The Free Press 1997.

Negroponte, Nicholas. *Being Digital*. New York: Alfred A. Knoph Inc., 1995.

O'Rourke, Michael. *Principals of Three-Dimensional Computer Animation: Modeling, Rendering, and Animating with 3D computer Graphics,* 2nd ed., New York: W.W. Norton & Co., 1998.

Packer, Randall and Jordon, Ken (eds.). *Multimedia: From Wagner to Virtual Reality*. New York: W.W. Norton & Co., 2000.

Paul, Christiane. *Digital Art*. London: Thames & Hudson Ltd., 2003.

Penny, Simon (ed.). *Critical Issues in Electronic Media*. Albany, NY: SUNY Press, 1995.

Popper, Frank. *Art of the Electronic Age*. London: Thames and Hudson, 1993.

Prophet, Jane. "TechnoSphere: 'Real' Time, 'Artificial' Life", *Leonardo* Vol. 34 No. 4, 2001, pp. 309–312.

Rinaldo, Kenneth (guest editor). Special Section. "Artificial Life Art", *Leonardo* Vol. 31 No. 5, 1998, pp. 370–406.

Rogala, Miroslaw with Moore, Darrel. "Nature is Leaving Us: A Video Theatre Work", *Leonardo* Vol. 26 No. 1, 1993, pp. 11–18.

Rush, Michael. *New Media in Late 20th-Century Art*. London: Thames and Hudson, 1999.

Russett, Robert and Starr, Cecile. *Experimental Animation: Origins of a New Art*. NewYork: Da Capo Press, 1988.

Schwartz, Lillian with Schwartz, Laurens R. *The Computer Artist's Handbook: Concepts, Techniques, and Applications*. New York: W.W. Norton, 1992.

Schwarz, Hans-Peter. *Media Art History*. Munich/New York: Prestal in association with the Media Museum, ZKM/Center for Art and Media (Karlsruhe, Germany), 1997.

Seaman, Bill. "Recombinant Poetics/VS/OULIPO", *Leonardo* Vol. 34 No. 5, 2001, pp. 423–430.

Shaw, Jeffrey. *a user's manual: From Expanded Cinema to Virtual Reality*. Karlsruhe, Germany: ZKM/Center for Art and Media Technology in association with Cantz Verlag, 1997.

_____and Weibel, Peter (eds.). *Future Cinema: The Cinematic Imaginary After Film*. Cambridge, MA: The MIT Press in association with ZKM/Center for Art and Media (Karlsruhe, Germany), 2003.

Sitney, P. Adams. *Visionary Film: The American Avant-Garde*. New York: Oxford University Press, 1974.

Solomon, Charles. *Enchanted Drawings: The History of Animation*. New York: Wings Books, 1994.

Sommerer, Christa with Mignonneau, Laurent. "Art as a Living System: Interactive Computer Artworks", *Leonardo* Vol. 32 No. 3, 1999, pp. 165–173.

_____. *Art @ Science*. New York: Springer-Verlag Wien, 1998.

Sorensen, Vibeke with Russett, Robert. "Computer Stereographics: The Coalescence of Virtual Space and Artistic Expression", *Leonardo* Vol. 32 No. 1 1999, pp. 41–48.

Starr, Cecile. *Discovering the Movies*. New York: Van Nostrand Reinhold, 1972.

Stauffacher, Frank (ed.). *Art in Cinema*. New York: Arno Press. (A Reprint of a 1947 San Francisco Museum of Art publication that includes articles, film notes and illustrations by and about Hans Richter, John and James Whitney, Fischinger, and others.)

Stephenson, Neal. *Snow Crash*. New York: Bantam Spectra, 1993.

Stephenson, Ralph. *Animation and the Cinema*. New York: Barnes and Company, 1967.

Sykes, Claire. "Futurism & Photography", *Photographer's Forum* Spring 2000, pp. 24–29.

Teilhard de Chardin, Pierre. *The Future of Man*. New York: Harper & Row, 1964.

Thomas, Frank and Johnston, Ollie. *Disney Animation: The Illusion of Life*. New York: Abbeville Press, 1981.

Todd, Stephen and Latham, William. *Evolutionary Art and Computers*. London: Academic Press, 1992.

Turkle, Sherry. "Who Am We", *WIRED*, January 1996, pp. 148–153.

Virilio, Paul. *The Vision Machine*. London: British Film Institute, 1994.

Vogel, Amos. *Film as a Subversive Art*. New York: Random House, 1974.

Whitelaw, Mitchell. *Metacreation: Art and Artificial Life*. Cambridge, MA: The MIT Press, 2004.

Whitney, John. *Digital Harmony, On the Complementarity of Music and Visual Art*. Peterborough, NH: Byte Books/McGraw-Hill, 1980.

_____. "Fifty Years of Composing Music and Graphics: How Time's New Solid-State Tractability Has Changed Audio-visual Perspectives", *Leonardo* Vol. 24

Youngblood, Gene. *Expanded Cinema*. New York: Dutton, 1970.

11 Acknowledgements

Thanks are due to a great many people who contributed to this book. To start, I owe an enormous debt of gratitude to the distinguished artists – twenty-three in all – who have provided interview material and who have generously shared their thoughts about Hyperanimation and frequently their visions of the future. Their help, enthusiasm and clear artistic insights into a complicated and ever evolving field were crucial to the thematic development of this book. Indeed, it would have been literally impossible to write and compile this volume without their cooperation. For this, one can only thank these artists formally and hope that the content of this book is illuminating and serves to incite yet further discourse.

In addition, I would like to acknowledge the assistance of those who have contributed in other important ways to making this project a reality. I am especially indebted to Silke Sutter of the Center for Art and Media (ZKM), who graciously arranged numerous interviews and provided essential background material. A consummate professional and good friend, Frau Sutter's generous support, patience and meticulous attention to detail were immensely helpful throughout the project. Special thanks are also due to Cecile Starr, whose encouragement and breath of knowledge about the art of animation were a great source of help and inspiration; Amanda Roth, publicist at Kleiser/Walczak, for kindly providing background information, arranging interviews and furnishing images pertaining to *Monsters of Grace*; Kathi Pavy for her contribution to the book's design; Professor Yeon Choi, who with patience and skill, helped manage the pesky technical problems associated with digital images and computer files, and Dr. Herbert Levine for his guidance, incisive advice and professional assistance. Most especially I wish to express my indebtedness and appreciation to my publisher John Libbey for taking on this project and for his cordial support and perceptive suggestions. His commitment to the project and his assiduous pursuit of excellence mark its every page.

There are a number of other people who deserve mention for their assistance and collegiality including Dean Gordon Brooks, Dr. Ray Authement and my former colleagues at the University of Louisiana at Lafayette; also the late Robert Mallary, Herman Mhire, Stewart McSherry, Barbara London (MoMA, NYC), Bruce Damer, Larry Cuba and Peter Weibel (ZKM). In addition, I would like to express my appreciation to the many artists who were interviewed, but not included in this volume. Their astute and thoughtful observations helped to broaden and inform the scope of this book.

Furthermore, I am grateful to the many individuals, families and organizations that contributed important documents, images and research materials. In addition to the twenty-three artists represented in these pages, I wish to thank Christopher A. Forte, Susan Emshwiller, Cecile Starr, Roger F. Malina and *LEONARDO*, John Whitney Jr. and the Estate of John and James Whitney, John Boesche, Bob Kuesel, Kleiser/Walczak and International Production Associates, Stephanie Berger, Chris Landreth and Alias/Wavefront, The Carnegie Museum of Art, Pittsburgh; Barbara Fischinger and The Elfrieda Fischinger Trust; Myron Krueger, Bill Viola, The Cooper Union School of Art, and The Len Lye Foundation, New Zealand.

I also wish to thank the various institutions and organizations that have provided assistance including the University of Louisiana at Lafayette, The Center for Art and Media (ZKM), Karlsruhe, Germany; The Edward MacDowell Colony, Peterborough, New Hampshire; SLEMCO, Lafayette, Louisiana; The Museum of Modern Art, NYC, the Electronic Visualization Laboratory (EVL), University of Illinois, Chicago; The Media Lab, Massachusetts Institute of Technology (MIT); Alias/Wavefront and The iotaCenter, Los Angeles, California.

Finally, I would like to thank my wife, Cecile DeVillier Russett, typist, proof reader, confidant and best friend for her unflagging patience and many sacrifices throughout this project. Her help, moral support, and unwavering belief in me were critically important to seeing this book through to completion.

Robert Russett *December 2008*

12 Indexes

NAMES

TITLES